FROM HELL TO ETERNITY

Life After Trauma

Phil Downer

with Susy, Paul, and Anna Downer

ETERNAL IMPACT PUBLISHING

Signal Mountain, Tennessee

From Hell to Eternity
Life After Trauma
Copyright © 2010 by Phil Downer

Published by Eternal Impact Publishing
Signal Mountain, TN 37377

First Edition

Library of Congress Control Number 2010920219

ISBN 9780578047706

Printed in China
10 11 12 13 / DH / 13 12 11 10

Cover Photos:
Top: U.S. Army Bell UH-1D helicopters airlift members of the 2nd Battalion, 14th Infantry Regiment during Operation "Wahiawa," South Viet Nam, 1966. James K. F. Dung, SFC, Photographer, Department of Defense.
Bottom, left: Phil Downer with his M-60 machine gun, Non Song, Viet Nam, 1967.
Bottom, center: Phil on patrol with his M-60 machine gun and Colt .45 automatic in a snake infested river near An Hoa, Viet Nam, 1967.
Bottom, right: Phil after an assault on a Viet Cong Vill, central highlands, Viet Nam, 1967.

TABLE OF CONTENTS

INTRODUCTION

As a Marine machine gunner in the rice paddies and jungle trails of Viet Nam, I underwent horrible trauma. No matter how life has dealt you its heaviest blows, I have found that such experiences leave their imprint deep in our memories and ways of thinking. Most of us do not take the time to reflect on these changes or understand the emotions and behaviors they produce in our lives. When reservoirs of pain, fear, or guilt boil up inside, we react out of instinct. We become angry, controlling, distrustful, depressed, overwhelmed, tense, or passive, expressing and medicating our inner turmoil as a reflex. Unless we learn to understand these deep hurts and discover the solutions to them, our days of war and combat will only continue, grow worse, and spread to others.

By the time I had reached my thirties, this is exactly what was taking place in my life. Despite my earnest attempts to cope with my wounds and find a cure for them, they continued to hemorrhage in my life and hurt the ones I loved the most, which only increased my sense of guilt and discouragement. Personally and professionally, I was becoming known for my explosive anger, defiant silences, critical tongue, and underlying lack of trust. My life experiences and training left me completely unprepared to be a loving husband, a caring father, a faithful friend, or a dependable worker.

The inner wounds I sustained in Viet Nam left me not only with deep scars, but also the mindset of one who is still in a war zone. At the same time, however, deep beneath my combative exterior, I longed more than anything for peace, gentle care, and a healing touch. But my hurt and resulting hardness had formed an impenetrable barrier between myself and others. I felt trapped by the way my life was turning out, and I was growing more doubtful every day that I would ever find a way to escape or start over. Then something amazing happened. I made a discovery that changed everything in my life.

As much as anyone else in the world, I am a guy who has zero interest in platitudes or clichés. But what I discovered wasn't a gimmick. It was the rescue I had been hoping for and my life has never been the same.

This story is not just my own. It is also the story of my wife, Susy, and our six children. Susy and two of our children, Paul and Anna, have contributed chapters to this book from their own perspectives. For Susy, the wounds I brought back from Viet Nam made her the inadvertent target of ambush over and over again during the early years of our marriage. For Paul and Anna, the ups and downs of my journey as a man were also the dominant shaping forces of their childhoods. They grew up as the children of a wounded father, a Viet Nam veteran suffering from Post-Traumatic Stress Disorder (PTSD). I went to war at the age of nineteen. They grew up in a post-war zone from the day they were born.

In a home where conflict, anger, and hurt were commonplace, a vibrant marriage and strong relationships with my children seemed impossible. But then, once again, against all odds, our lives began to change. The wonderful friendship and closeness we enjoy today are living proof that miracles truly do still happen. Not only was my broken marriage beautifully restored, but I also experienced the joy of reconciliation with the next generation in my family.

No matter what traumatic or painful things have happened to you, or what you have done as a result, I know from experience that radical change is possible—and not just for me. It is possible for you as well. I have seen the concepts and truths contained in this book transform tens of thousands of lives over the years since they first impacted mine. Our family is not special. We are normal, broken people who have experienced deep and lasting change in our lives to no credit of our own. I want that kind of transformation to enter your life and relationships as well.

Our hope is that the vulnerable sharing of our lives contained in these pages will be an encouragement to you, and that by walking with us through our struggles, mistakes, and the discoveries that changed our lives, you too might experience peace of mind, restored relationships, and newness of life.

Phil Downer

May 1, 2010

SPECIAL TRIBUTE

Iwould like to offer a special tribute to Ralph Crossley, who trained me as a Marine machine gunner, fought with me in combat, and saved my life in the heat of battle more than once. Ralph stood as best man in my wedding and has continued to stand with me through the hard times and the good times since. Cross, without you, this book, my family, and the last 42 years of my life never would have been. Words cannot express the debt of gratitude I owe you. Semper Fi, brother.

Phil Downer

Left, Ralph Crossley
Right, Phil Downer
An Hoa, Viet Nam, 1967

CHAPTER ONE

Combat Grief

Mosquitoes so big they reminded me of the helicopters constantly buzzing overhead. Humidity that stuck my clothes to my body like glue. The presence of danger so close, so real, even sleep didn't provide any respite, much less peace. Like all Marines, I had learned to rest lightly, ready to spring into action at the first "snap!" of a twig or burst of machine gun fire.

In the spring of 1967, South Viet Nam didn't make the top ten list of the world's best vacation destinations. Yet there I was, along with thousands of other American men and women, determined to help turn back the Communist forces from the north. Despite my bravado, I desperately hoped somehow just to come home in one piece.

After a brief and unsuccessful stay in the picturesque college town of Athens, I had flunked out of Ohio University. I worked in an aircraft factory during the summer of 1966 before enlisting in the United States Marine Corps. After basic training, I went to Camp Pendleton in California where battle-hardened Marines taught me jungle warfare. Then they shipped me off to

Viet Nam where I served as an infantry machine gunner in Hotel Company, 2nd Battalion, 5th Marines.

Though I was a fresh-faced, wide-eyed nineteen-year-old kid, I was convinced I was tough and cool. Growing up, I used to watch war movies where the Marines landed on beaches and charged up the hills of those islands in the Pacific. I remember rooting silently as a rugged John Wayne led his troops to victory. He was my hero. Now I figured I was just like him: trained, strong, and ready for anything.

I also thought I was tough because machine gunners have one of the shortest life expectancies of anyone in combat. In an infantry platoon, the machine gunner commands overwhelming firepower. So, naturally, the enemy tries to zero in on him. Their first priority is to knock the machine gunner out of battle and neutralize his weapon. Did that bother me? Not a bit. I wore this bulls-eye like a badge of honor that proved my superiority. But that was pre-deployment while I was still in California!

After landing in the northern part of South Viet Nam, it didn't take long for me to lose my grand ideas about combat. I was soon harshly confronted with a very basic fact—John Wayne had lied in all those movies. He had always made combat look fun, like it was the kind of rush that any red-blooded American would want to experience. Nothing could have been further from the truth.

In my outfit, the up-close, gut-wrenching killing and dying took place day in and day out. Watching my dying buddies as they suffered in agony was an experience I will never forget. It was terrible beyond description. Killing the enemy didn't make it feel any better. It was just one more painful dimension of the horrors of war.

A Marked Man

I will never forget one particular day at the beginning of Operation Essex that shook me to the core of my soul. It was

November 6, 1967. Our superiors ordered our company to lead the first stage of a helicopter assault—a search-and-destroy mission into an area known as Antenna Valley. It was so called because of the extremely high number of radio men who had been among the casualties of the most recent battles in the region.

The valley was positioned at the heart of the infamous Ho Chi Minh Trail, the crucial supply line for the North Vietnamese Army moving south. Since the enemy had turned it into a stronghold, it represented a virtual no-man's land for American military personnel. We had been assigned the daunting task of carrying out an assault that was designed to drive the enemy out of this key objective and turn it over to our forces.

An hour before sunrise we boarded helicopters, their blades rhythmically slicing the tension-filled air. As we piled on and took our places, squeezing our weapons between our knees, I could see it on every face—we had no doubt that some of the men sitting with us would not make it back. With a roar, the choppers tore into the sky, banked sharply, and then leaned forward as they rushed us into the teeth of the coming battle. Our minds raced as our adrenaline kicked into overdrive. The minutes passed like hours.

Just as the sun peeked over the horizon, our long line of choppers dipped sharply out of the sky and flew in low and fast, straight up the mouth of Antenna Valley. The choppers touched down quickly, lingering in the landing zone only long enough for us to rush to the door and leap to the ground before they lifted off and climbed steeply back into the sky. Keeping our heads as low as we could, we mustered into our teams and began to charge across an open rice paddy toward the tree line, hoping to spring a surprise attack.

This time, the surprise was on us.

Concealed from view and armed with automatic weapons loaded and ready to fire, the enemy waited in complete silence as we approached their battle lines. We had no idea that hundreds of enemy soldiers were silently training their weapons on us and carefully choosing their targets as we charged directly into what we called "the kill zone"—a deadly area where automatic weapon fire sweeps left and right in crisscrossing patterns, decimating everything in its path.

Just as my company hit the rice paddy, the tree line dead in front of us erupted with an explosion of automatic weapon fire, mowing us down like a scythe cutting through blades of grass. The initial barrage of small arms fire was so focused and overwhelming that within the first ninety seconds, more than twenty-five percent of my company was dead or wounded.

The shock and chaos was horrific. As I flattened my body against the ground, my ears were filled with the deadly popping sound of bullets zipping past just inches above our heads. We were trapped. We radioed for air strikes and within minutes, F-4s and Crusader jets thundered in, dropping their payloads of bombs and napalm so close to our position that the explosions bounced us off the ground like rubber balls, nearly tossing us into the paths of the bullets that were slicing through the air just above us.

Artillery from our firebase in An Hoa screamed over us as it hurtled toward the enemy's position. But these counter-attacks didn't help us much. We were pinned down within shouting distance of the enemy, who continued to rain down small arms fire directly into our position.

Our helicopters couldn't retrieve our dead and wounded, and with machine gun fire ripping through their undersides like tin cans, the choppers had no choice but to pull back and peel off from such a hot LZ (landing zone). Reluctantly, our support forces had to leave us there to "gut it out" without reinforcements. Seeking to relieve some of the pressure on our position, my platoon planned a movement around the left flank.

By this time, I had been in Viet Nam about six months and was no longer the machine gunner. On the basis of combat performance and the attrition due to battlefield casualties, I had been promoted. Just a few days before coming to Antenna Valley, I had moved up to being the machine gun team leader. I had passed my weapon to John Atkinson, an excellent gunner about my age, who had been promoted into my old position as machine gunner. As we followed our orders to charge around the left flank, I led the team with an M-16 assault rifle clenched in my hands at the ready, with John following several feet behind.

We charged in single file, crossed to the other side of the rice paddy, and reached a covered trail where we made a sharp left-hand turn. As soon as John hit the trail, enemy fire poured down on us. Immediately, we dropped to the ground to return fire. As I hit the deck, I felt an AK-47 bullet pierce my backpack from behind. It tore through the bottom of my pack and out the top, just missing the back of my head. The impact shattered my extra pair of eyeglasses and exploded my C-rations, throwing me down hard.

Just then, I felt something heavy strike my leg. Immediately, I rolled over. It was my old machine gun. And John. It only took a moment to realize that, except for the bullet that had passed harmlessly through my backpack, all the other bullets had struck my friend. Though I felt sure he had died before hitting the ground, I instantly called for a medic, screaming, "Corpsman up! Corpsman up!"

Crouching with my fallen comrade in my hands and lap, a wave of pain washed over me as I watched the blood from his bullet-riddled body drip onto my uniform. I felt like someone had ripped my stomach out.

As the horror of the fact that John was dead sank in, it just seemed so wrong to me. Not only was John my friend, he was one of the finest Marines in our outfit. Unlike the foul-mouthed, hard-drinking Marines that surrounded him, I never heard him swear or say a bad thing about anyone. This All-American hero loved his family, constantly talking about them and his new wife, whom he had just learned was pregnant with their first child.

The Corpsman checked for a pulse, confirming what I already knew. John would never hear the word "Daddy." He was one of our very best, a hero from New York—and now he was gone, dead in my arms.

Though the enemy had seen us dart across the rice paddy and onto the trail, they had patiently waited for the rest of us to pass before opening fire on the machine gunner. Three days earlier, I would have been carrying the machine gun. But because of my promotion, and John's, the gun had passed to my friend— along with a death sentence.

The realization hit me like a ton of bricks: John had taken *my place* in death.

I had no idea how to process the feelings of loss, pain, and guilt that were twisting inside of me. All these thoughts and emotions swept over me in a matter of moments, but no matter how badly any of us felt about losing our fellow warriors and friends in combat, we knew we had to go on. In the midst of the fierceness of this battle, I found myself back on machine gun duty, taking the place in life of the one who had taken my place in death.

From that time on, I have been a marked man. It is something that has impacted my life every single day for more than 40 years. It still seems like yesterday.

Survival Prayer

That night, I was in a fire position overlooking a rice paddy dike with another great Marine, my dear friend and fellow machine gunner, Ralph Crossley. When I arrived, Ralph was the best machine gunner in our company. He trained me and I trained John. Ralph had saved my life and I had saved his. He was and is one of my life heroes. Crouched behind that dike, we leaned on our elbows so we could fire over it without needlessly exposing ourselves to enemy fire. Because the battle had been so fierce, there hadn't been a spare minute to dig a foxhole for protection. What was left of our company had stationed themselves behind us while we held the highest point with the least amount of cover.

At about midnight, our already precarious situation took a drastic turn for the worse. The enemy circled around behind us and attacked our position. With our flanks completely exposed and the dike in front of us now useless as cover from the enemy to our rear, there was little we could do to protect ourselves. Unable to return fire, I felt helpless. If I raised up to shoot in front of me, I would make myself a target for bullets coming from behind, and I was so tightly pinned down by fire from the rear, maneuvering to return fire in that direction was impossible as well. We were bunched so close together with the enemy, I couldn't even tell which positions were ours and which were theirs. Though I could easily hear and see the muzzle flashes, I had no way of knowing who was firing at whom.

The only thing Ralph and I could do was hug the ground, staying as low as we could while the worst firestorm I had ever experienced continued to rage over and all around us. Incoming bullets struck the ground so close to me that they sprayed dirt clods against my helmet and flak jacket. Overhead we heard high-powered rifle bullets zipping past, cracking like the pop-pop-pop of popcorn heating in a cooker. We lay there, anticipating at any moment that the very next *pop*! might be the end of us. This was the first time that I couldn't fight back while under attack. Completely trapped and surrounded, I seriously thought my life was about to end.

This helpless feeling lasted only a few seconds, but it seemed like many long minutes as we savored each anxious breath. I remember thinking back to how I had goofed my way through high school and then flunked out of college. "This is it," I thought, gritting my teeth. "There is no tomorrow. No make-up tests. No next semester. It's all over."

Right then I said my "foxhole prayer." Lying face down on the ground with hell breaking loose all around me, I pleaded with God. As my friends in real estate say, I was ready to deal. As the sounds of explosions and dying men rang out all around me, I whispered into the blackness, "God, if you get me out of this, I'll do anything. I'll go back and make something of my life. I'll join a church. I'll become a Christian. Just let me make it out of here alive."

Honestly, I'm not sure what prompted me to say those things. I might have been trying to impress God. After all, when your life hangs in the balance, you're willing to say or try just about anything. But at that moment, it wasn't just talk. I was serious. I realized the way I had been living had taken me down the wrong path. I was out of options.

These desperate thoughts covered only a few moments and then Ralph screamed, "Downer I'm hit!" I crawled over to Crossley, expecting to see blood and torn flesh. Thankfully I found only a torn shirt! A bullet had ripped through the sleeve under Crossley's armpit and hit the ground beneath him with so much force it had flipped him over like a dead fish. But dead he wasn't, and I have been forever thankful he so narrowly escaped being counted among the good men who died that day.

God answered my prayer for protection that night. Ralph and I finally escaped that crisis as our Marine unit overpowered the enemy and forced them to draw back. By about 1 a.m., the action had finally faded into stillness. For a few hours, there weren't any bullets popping overhead. We could breathe a sigh of relief.

Now, I can't say that escaping with my life turned me into a spiritual seeker. But though I didn't know God, I felt a general sense that I had been spared. For some unknown reason, I knew that Something or Someone up above had enabled me to survive another horrifying, life-threatening situation. I believed this Force would spare me in others yet to come.

The next morning, helicopters swarmed in with new rations. As photo crews from NBC News hopped off to take film of our dead buddies, I was so full of hurt I felt like gunning them down. As soon as the choppers unloaded their cargo of food, we loaded them up again with dead Marines in body bags. Soon they would return with replacements from the rear so we could proceed with the remainder of the operation.

In November of 2007, *Leatherneck Magazine* published an article on Operation Essex that offers a first-hand account of what this battle scene looked like from the sky. Captain David Marshall, "a highly skilled and completely fearless aviator,"[1] was a well known A-4 Skyhawk attack pilot who was on duty that fateful day. When Hotel Company got caught in the teeth of the vicious surprise attack that had been launched just moments after Operation Essex began, it lost radio contact with its parent battalion in the rear.

As the hours of radio silence dragged on, Captain Marshall and his co-pilot, Lieutenant Robert Whitlow, were called upon to fly a spotter plane into Antenna Valley to determine our location and condition. Headed for the coordinates of our last known position, Whitlow recalls that Antenna Valley was covered by a layer of low-lying fog that wound up the valley like a "thick, white, fuzzy caterpillar."[2] It was obvious to both of them that getting low enough to get a visual of Hotel Company was going to be risky. *Leatherneck Magazine* reported:

> Marshall said, "Hold on, Rob, this is going to get interesting," and put the aircraft into a dive through the impenetrable fog. Whitlow could see no visual reference point, and only the rapidly unwinding altimeter told them how high they were. Marshall worked under the fog and flew along the Thu Bon River just a few feet above its muddy surface.[3]

Then, suddenly, they came upon the scene where our battle had been the previous day.

1. LtCol Otto J. Lehrack, USMC (Ret) "Operation Essex: The NVA Chose to Fight in Antenna Valley—They Died," Leatherneck Magazine 24, 26 (Nov. 2007).
2. Ibid.
3. Ibid.

Whitlow and Marshall agreed that it was the single worst sight either of them had seen in Viet Nam. Whitlow said it could have been a scene from Dante's "Inferno." The terrain was completely devastated, and they saw the survivors grouped together in a tight perimeter atop a hill. Bodies were everywhere—both Marines and NVA [North Vietnamese Army]. Whitlow called in air strikes to pound the surrounding terrain in case any NVA remained in the area.[4]

A Lifestyle of Fear

This was not the only time we suffered massive losses. Many times in Viet Nam, we headed off into battle and returned with only two thirds of our machine gunners. If twenty machine gunners went out, we came back with twelve. As soon as I got close to a young Marine who needed me to help him learn about combat, we were loading him into a chopper covered in blood. After each battle, a supply of fresh faces joined us. We would try to convey confidence, only to go out and get cut into pieces again and again. It was a devastating way of life.

As I continued to return from each of these bloody firefights unscathed, it began to haunt me. One day another friend, J.D. Majors, took over my machine gun. Because of a change in the prescription for my military glasses, the doctor had placed drops in my eyes to dilate them and I couldn't go out on maneuvers for twelve hours. My friend J.D. said, "Hey Downer, I'll go," and took my machine gun on that patrol—my patrol. He stepped on a land mine and lost an eye and an arm.

As the days and weeks passed, fear became my uninvited and constant companion. We did our jobs, but we braved each new trail and unknown village with both courage and trepidation. We especially feared booby traps. The enemy would take duds—live munition rounds that had failed to explode—and string them together with little trip wires and bury them. The triggers, or trip wires, were impossible to see through a thicket

4. Ibid.

of underbrush. Often, as we cleared or swept through an area, a booby trap would go off and take one or more men apart.

I'll never forget watching in horror as my buddy, Willie, stepped on a booby trap directly in front of me. The explosion threw him into the air as his body splattered into pieces before my eyes. He fell to the ground with both legs gone. "God, please let me die," he cried. "Don't help me!" he yelled, as we rushed to get help from a medical corpsman. "Don't send me back to my wife like this! Let me die!" he screamed.

As we carried the half of his body that remained to the medical helicopter, we tried to lift his spirits and keep him conscious by talking to him and handing him $20 bills, yelling over the din of the chopper blades, "This is for a night on the town when you get back!" "Buy a steak on me!" Though Willie lifted off with hundreds of dollars in cash clenched in his trembling hands, we knew that no amount of money could buy back his legs or change what was ahead of him.

Though I felt Willie's anguish in the pit of my stomach, there was a sense in which I didn't pity his condition. True, his legs were gone—and more. But at least he knew he was probably going to make it home alive. "For him," I thought, "Nam is over." Most of us would have eagerly traded places with him because of the unseen foes we knew we still had to face with no guarantee of surviving. It may have been selfish of me, but in a twisted way I envied him. For Willie, the war and the constant fear were finally over, but for me it would continue.

To my shock, it would continue for decades in my heart and soul.

Home Is Where the Hurt Is

After many more months of gruesome combat, the day finally came in the spring of 1968 when I got to go home. At last, there were no more bombs dropping around us, no more bullets flying by our heads, no more body bags to load. What a relief. As I took off on that plane from Viet Nam, I purposed never to fight anyone again.

When I touched down on U.S. soil, however, conditions weren't what we had anticipated while passing anxious hours in those rice paddies. We had hoped to return to a country that welcomed us as brave men who had fought to keep America free. No celebrations greeted our arrival, however. No bands marched ahead of us in parades. Because of the unpopularity of the Viet Nam War, we came home to indifference and at times, hostility.

I didn't expect a hero's welcome. I was no hero, though I had served with some real heroes. I didn't get a medal for my courage and I wasn't even wounded. Not physically, at least. My reward was going home. I did the job my country called me to do. I did it well, with precision and courage. I had the respect of the men with whom I served.

Yet, I never remember even one person on the street, in the airport, or a restaurant saying anything approaching, "Thanks for serving our country." Burned in my heart was the face of a well-dressed, sweet-looking young mom, who saw me coming through the airport gate in my uniform and pulled her children away from me like I was some kind of monster.

After my hair grew out and I got comfortable wearing jeans again, I looked like any other college boy walking down the street. I hadn't lost any limbs, but my heart and soul were pierced with the pain and horror of a war that still raged within me. I was filled with raw, war-scorched emotions and a guilt-ridden spirit because I had survived when better men had not. I carried a deep sense that no one cared about me. I felt blamed for everything and credited for nothing. I determined that I would get even. I would achieve and I would succeed and no one would ever again have the nerve to say to me, "You lost the war."

All of us returning vets went through the shunning and spitting in the airports. The hardest thing for me, however, was walking away one night from some soft, vulgar frat boys who called me the enemy and a baby killer and threw beer in my face. Little did they know how close they came to death that night as I visualized how I would crush one of their skulls with the half-full long neck Bud I held in my left hand and take out another with the pizza knife on the nearby table. The third clown was so drunk he probably would have fallen over with one push. I was a bitter young man boiling with hurt and hatred.

But I thought, "No, my war is over. I'm headed to college to make top grades. I must once again take the painful humiliation of a bunch of civilians who could never measure up to even one John Atkinson."

The icy homecoming was bad enough, but that was only the beginning of my hardships stateside. Before going to Viet Nam, many of us vets had flunked out of college or not earned the grades in high school even to apply. We hoped our service in Southeast Asia would count for something, but for thousands of us, it seemed to carry little weight.

Since my family had moved to Dallas, I began looking at colleges in that area. Their pre-admission interviews were a piece of cake, and my references were fairly strong. When they came across my grades and resulting dismissal from Ohio University, however, they quickly lost interest. Granted, I had flunked Algebra twice during two consecutive semesters, mainly because I never got out of bed early enough for my 8 a.m. class. But couldn't a guy get a break? Didn't active military service and several years of maturity count for anything?

It looked like John Wayne hadn't just lied about the thrill of combat. There wasn't much glory in this "welcome home" either.

Questions For Reflection

1. What was a deep pain you suffered before you were 20 years old?

2. How have you felt rejected or neglected?

3. Who is your hero?

4. Whose hero are you?

5. What is one thing in your past you would want to relive?

6. What is one thing in your past you would not want to relive?

CHAPTER TWO

Upwardly Mobile

Despite the many disappointments I endured during my post-Viet Nam round of college admission visits, I refused to give up on what I had promised in my foxhole prayer—to make something of my life. I finally came across a junior college that had just opened in downtown Dallas, and I applied. El Centro Junior College accepted me as a member of its first-year class. Considering my alternatives, I was thrilled to be able to study there.

Life As a Student

Adjusting to campus life again wasn't easy. Frequently, as I crossed campus with a heavy load of books on my back, I would flash back to the torn bodies of my screaming buddies as we carried them to choppers in such high numbers that, at many points, I couldn't lift my arms.

As the flashbacks continued, I found myself struggling with a poor attention span and a limited ability to focus. I tried to find a measure of relief and happiness by what I drank and who I was with, but it didn't help. Sometimes in the middle of trying to analyze and solve a test problem, everything in me would suddenly want to be violent. I was also disturbed by the way people splashed barbecue sauce on burnt pork at cookouts, which smelled just like Willie's legs—or rather what was left of his legs after he had hit the booby trap.

Despite these obstacles, I buckled down this time and really hit the books. Not only was I older now, but the time I had spent in combat had given me a much-needed dose of reality. Motivated to work hard and apply myself, I realized that to move on from El Centro, I would have to make straight A's, or close to it. And I did just that.

After a year, I applied to Southern Methodist University. Despite my poor marks from Ohio University, the admissions officer decided to take a chance on me. The first time we met, he remarked that when he had reviewed my transcript, he had assumed English was my second language because my English SAT scores were so low. After talking with me and seeing my sincerity and resolve, and perhaps my Marine service, he said the very words I had been hoping to hear for months: "OK, I'll let you in. You don't deserve it with your grades, but I think you've changed. Don't let me down."

With visions of how I had flunked out of Ohio University lingering in my head, I realized that getting admitted to SMU didn't guarantee I would remain there. I concentrated on my studies and, fortunately, earned excellent grades once again. Quality education was not the only benefit to be found there, however.

Love and Loneliness

In an economics class one day, I met the woman of my dreams, Susy Olschner. We felt an immediate attraction for each other, and after dating throughout our junior year, we were married. Since we both had our eyes set on the legal field, we applied to a number of law schools and settled on Emory University School of Law, primarily because we loved the city of Atlanta.

I was blessed with a wife who had never been yelled at in her life, had undying optimism, and slept soundly. So, as the horrors of what I had experienced in battle continued to haunt me, especially at night, she would often lay peacefully undisturbed when I would wake up screaming, in a cold sweat, reliving the battles where so many good men had died.

As hard as she tried to understand me, my new wife was completely bewildered by the war that was raging inside of me. During law school, when my wife and I watched the fall of Saigon on TV, with people hanging off the helicopter atop the U.S. Embassy, Susy muttered some words of inevitability and went to bed. I stayed up all night and stared at the wall and cried. As much as she might have wanted to, she just couldn't understand.

However constructive the intention, I would take Susy's periodic comments of criticism as personal attacks. I would explode with venomous anger, hurling and crushing furniture and spewing obscenities in rage. When powerful waves of depression, sadness, and pain would grip me and I took it out on her, she would shout back at me, "I'm not your enemy! I'm not your enemy!"

As those early months and years of marriage passed, we fought more and more. When our fights would come to an end, I would apologize to Susy. Sometimes, however, I felt not only numb about what I had said and done, but also fully justified in being verbally aggressive due to my own sense of being attacked by Susy's criticism. Despite reaching our goals of graduating from college and getting into a good law school together, our marriage was quickly falling apart.

I didn't know it at the time, but Susy was considering divorce—a thought which had entered her mind the first time I flew into a rage the second night of our honeymoon. Hoping that my temperament would improve after the pressure of law school was behind us, Susy put off her plans for divorce.

Professional Success, Private Heartache

After graduating from Emory, we started our professional careers. I joined a wonderful, small, up-and-coming law firm downtown, and Susy got a fabulous job in the legal department of Delta Air Lines. I worked for two terrific lawyers who cared for me and were excited about helping me begin my legal career.

But once again, I discovered that my old buddy, John Wayne, had lied. Whenever he wasn't charging into combat and winning dramatic battles, his movies portrayed worldly success, romantic love, a prestigious job, family, a house, and money in the bank as the source of fulfillment in life.

After surviving Viet Nam, overcoming my initial college failures, finding and winning the woman of my dreams, and becoming a key player in a growing law firm, I expected my life to be everything I'd ever wanted it to be. My experience, however, was just the opposite. The more goals I met, the more empty I became.

Soon, even my law office felt like a prison. When the bank helicopter would fly between the towers outside my window to pick up the bank checks, I would zone out for five seconds, or sometimes five minutes, my heart pounding, back rigid, and my fist and jaw clenched before it would finally sink in that I was not going in for another attack where my friends were going to die.

I remembered thinking to myself over and over in Viet Nam, "If I only had one hot meal a day, six hours of sleep a night, and no one trying to blow me away, then I would never want for another thing." I especially wanted to live that way because John and my other fallen buddies couldn't. But now I had all of that and so much more, but I was no happier than when I had been on those jungle paths.

When I spewed out rage toward Susy, I felt tremendous guilt toward my buddies. I felt that, if they had lived, they would have done a much better job than I was doing with the gift of life.

Though I continued to struggle with frequent nighttime returns to the horrors of battle, I faced even bigger struggles during my waking hours, trying to deal with people who didn't understand my short fuse, care about my lost friends, or have any comprehension of the throbbing emptiness and aloneness that I felt.

Some days I even wanted to go back to Viet Nam. I hated war, but I was trained for it. I wasn't trained to handle post-war life with a bunch of soft, ungrateful civilians. I thought that over there, my inner war would have been understood.

I tried to overcome my temptation to apathy through obsessive over-achieving, compulsiveness, and perfectionism. But this only compounded my problems. I simply had no place to put my anger, fear, hurt, guilt, false guilt, loneliness, sense of rejection, and deep-seated malaise of failure.

Though I had led men in combat with courage and reached a measure of success in the business world, I collided with failure every day just trying to be kind and gentle to my wife whom I desperately loved with all my heart. My problems were so beyond my control that I couldn't even keep from destroying my relationship with the single person in the world who was most precious to me.

I hoped that my explosions of anger and impatience would be erased by the good times Susy and I shared together. But they never were. Though few could spot it from the outside, I felt adrift, lonely, restless, and unfulfilled. While I did experience some happy moments, they were fleeting. Barely a day went by that I didn't think to myself, "What am I missing?" "Where did I go wrong?" "I'm no good." "Life just isn't worth it."

I had accumulated all the ingredients of the Great American Dream, but each day seemed to me more like the Great American Nightmare. As our fights continued with killing frequency, Susy was quickly reaching the same conclusion. Our home was filled with tension, bickering, and defensiveness. To put it more accurately, I argued with Susy. No matter the situation, I always thought I was right.

When we were married, I had very little self-awareness. But being married taught me a lot about what I was like. I was arrogant, self-centered, insensitive, stubborn, impatient, and prone to swing back and forth between laziness and workaholism. As the fourth year of our marriage became a fifth, it was clear that our marriage was dying a slow and painful death.

Trouble at the Office

My character flaws were not confined to my home life. At the office, the two fine law partners who had hired me soon began to notice these malignant qualities, too. They wanted me to succeed, of course. They had made a major capital investment in starting their firm and developing a growing client list. They were building a reputation as professionals and felt I had the abilities to help the firm grow.

Since attorneys don't have the benefit of internships or residencies like doctors, my partners were willing to devote time and effort to correcting my inevitable on-the-job mistakes. Soon I was performing with a high level of success in courtroom litigation and was gaining a reputation as an excellent attorney.

My temperamental outbursts were increasing in frequency, however. I was changing from being a valuable asset to an unpredictable liability. Being a trial lawyer began to feel a lot like being in Viet Nam. I proceeded down jungle trails of jurisprudence, never knowing when or from where someone might ambush me.

Sometimes a witness would take the stand and suddenly forget everything we had reviewed the day before. A client would not show up for court, or a judge would decide to postpone a case when I finally had my experts, evidence, and case assembled. Or an opposing lawyer might suddenly demolish one of the key elements of my case and leave me scrambling to pick up the pieces.

Such unknowns were a constant source of tension for me and I radiated that inner stress and pressure toward those around me.

My welcome at the firm was quickly wearing thin.

Empty Religion

During this time I followed through on the second part of my foxhole-prayer. I joined a church. Susy and I chose it based on its architectural appeal. We liked its quaint, old English style and figured that once you step through the door, most churches were pretty much the same anyway. When we met some nice people who really seemed to care about us, our assumption seemed justified.

We did more than join the church. We got involved. When we were asked to take charge of the youth program, we accepted, taking young people on various outings and service projects. When someone asked me to teach Sunday school, it became a forum for expressing my opinions on political and social issues. Since a lot of members patted me on the back, I thought I must be doing a pretty good job.

In time, I even agreed to take a seat on the church's governing board, helping make decisions about the minister, the property, the programs, and other administrative concerns.

Though it was enjoyable, I had a new problem. Instead of spending six days a week at the office, I was now working seven. I had more committees, more people to please, more stress in my life, and less fulfillment than ever.

I wasn't finding any peace in religion.

At the end of a long day of work at the office or church, I would come home wanting nothing more than to find a haven of safety, comfort, and understanding—an escape from the chaos and tensions of everyday life. We had purchased a picture-perfect, two-bedroom house about fifteen minutes from downtown Atlanta, located in a neighborhood with nice neighbors and tall pine trees. Despite all of this, home was anything but a haven for

Susy and me. Day after day, I left the perfect job to return to the perfect house and the perfect wife, still burdened by all the troubles, frustrations, fears, and anxieties that I had accumulated at work. I would then dump these on Susy, and the loveless nights of fighting would start all over again.

I didn't like the person I had become, but I didn't have the ability to change. Why hadn't anyone told me that the American Dream was a sham, a bitter joke? I had everything I had ever wanted in life and all it brought me was misery, restlessness, and a burning hunger inside that I couldn't explain or extinguish.

Being an ex-Marine, a real tough guy, I often expressed these feelings in physical ways. We had a captain's chair in storage in our attic, its arms lying in pieces around it. I had broken them in anger, glued them back on, and then broken them off again. Over time, we amassed an attic full of the furniture that I had destroyed. On the wall over our kitchen phone, there were dents where I had smashed the receiver during a conversation that hadn't gone to my liking. The dashboard of my car bore knuckle marks, a sign of the encouragement I had offered an elderly driver who had been struggling to maneuver through rush-hour traffic one day.

Though Susy was never the target of my physical wrath, my actions terrified her, and my harsh, angry words wounded her, destroying the love she had for me piece by piece. As hard as I tried, I couldn't figure out what had gone wrong. Even though I had everything I had ever dreamed of having, all I had to show for it was a life-sized supply of turmoil. One day I thought about my desperate prayer in Viet Nam. I had made three promises that day:

1) To go home and make something of myself

2) To join a church

3) To become a Christian

I had gone above and beyond in keeping the first two promises. But I recognized I had failed to keep the third. Though I hadn't been raised in a spiritually devout family, I knew that despite reaching some professional achievements, the real me hadn't changed.

I knew that truly becoming a Christian was something that should make a difference in my life. Yes, I had visited a lot of places that were called "Christian," and I had even called myself one. But God had never become personal to me or had seemingly changed anything about who I was.

Looking for Help

I sensed I needed to do something, but I didn't know where to go or who to talk to. I didn't know anyone who was all that different from me. Most people at church seemed to have the same problems I did. They would battle with their problems all week, come to a Sunday service, hear some nice words, say they were sorry, and go home to repeat the cycle. Deep down I knew we had to be missing something.

Meanwhile, Susy had begun meeting with a woman named Liane to study the Bible. They eventually convinced me to attend a CBMC luncheon where a successful businessman from Detroit was to speak.

During his talk, Paul Johnson (now a mentor and close friend) made some interesting comments about his business experience and achievements. He said that the foundation and driving force in his life was not professional success, but a personal relationship with God through Jesus Christ; that this is what had brought him an inner peace like nothing he had found anywhere else. This was the first time I had ever heard of such a concept. To me, God seemed distant, mysterious, and unknowable.

Not only did Paul talk about having a personal relationship with God, he pointed out that it was accessible to everyone, not just to people who had their lives together or who were special somehow. He explained that personal friendship and peace with God was a gift, available for the asking at any time to everyone.

Paul quoted a Bible verse that said, "Behold, I stand at the door and knock. If anyone hears My voice and opens the door, I will come in to him and dine with him, and he with Me" (Rev. 3:20). This sounded so simple to me it seemed almost unbelievable, but it really got me thinking.

Paul's talk impacted me in a deep way. It was the first time I had heard anyone, other than a clergyman, speak with conviction about God. Though I had just met him, I could tell that Paul was speaking from his heart. It impressed me that, as a businessman, he talked openly about Jesus Christ because he wanted to, not because it was part of his job description.

The strongest impression he made on me was that despite his many pressures and responsibilities, he talked about having a peace in his life that I could not even imagine. He shared some verses from the book of Romans, chapter 5, verses 6-8, which read, "You see, at just the right time, when we were still powerless, Christ died for the ungodly. Very rarely will anyone die for a righteous man, though for a good man someone might possibly dare to die. But God demonstrates his own love for us in this: While we were still sinners, Christ died for us."

These verses made something click for me. For the first time in my life, my heart screamed with the recognition that Jesus Christ had come to earth and died *for me!* He took my bullets just as John had. But Jesus had done so voluntarily.

I didn't deserve to have Him do this for me, any more than I deserved to have John take over my machine gun and become the primary target of enemy snipers. I recognized for the first time that I could be free of my sin and guilt by accepting what Jesus had done for me, just like I had been able to walk away from death the day John had died in my place.

Searching for Meaning and Truth

I didn't respond immediately, but hearing what Paul shared was the beginning of a new chapter in my life. My training as a lawyer prompted me to begin a more thorough study of the evidence. I began examining the Bible much like I would examine relevant documents for an upcoming trial.

This led me to some interesting verses, including Romans 3:23, which says that every person is guilty of doing wrong and falling short of God's perfect standard. As an ex-party boy and Marine, I had no problem with that idea. I knew I was a big-time sinner.

I also saw that my pride, arrogance, impatience, and anger had created barriers, not only with my wife and employers, but also with God. That was a sobering realization to me. But I found encouragement in another verse which said, "the wages of sin is death, but the free gift of God is eternal life in Christ Jesus our Lord" (Romans 6:23).

As part of my search, I also began meeting with a man named Jim Lyon. Jim was a doctor who hated lawyers, but he loved me. As a business professional, he was another guy I could relate to who had a genuine relationship with God. He began to spend time with me over a weekly breakfast.

He went over verses from the Bible, explaining who God is and showing me passages like 1 John 5:11-13, which reads, "And this is the testimony: God has given us eternal life, and this life is in his Son. He who has the Son has life; he who does not have the Son of God does not have life. I write these things to you who believe in the name of the Son of God so that you may know that you have eternal life."

Soon after we began meeting together, a lawyer in my office invited me to go on a Christian men's retreat. I declined, listing all my church obligations and explaining that I didn't need any more religion. Though I had a burning desire to learn more about what it meant to truly be a Christian, a retreat sounded like just one more activity.

Several days later, Susy asked me an unusual question: "Phil, have I ever asked you to do something just for me?" I paused for a moment and thought about it. We had one of those "equal" marriages where we never imposed on each other. During our five years together, my wife had never asked me to do something without providing additional reasons and explanations. I had to admit, "No, I don't think you ever have."

"Would you go on this retreat, Phil? For me?"

"Well," I said, "if it's that important to you, I guess I'll go. What's three days?"

It wasn't until years later that I learned what a deep sense of desperation had been behind Susy's request. Though she had by then seriously been considering divorce for some time, she thought something good might happen if I went on this men's retreat. She didn't hold out much hope, but she was willing to give it a try. This was her last resort.

The day the retreat was to start, I drove to a church where I encountered a group of men I had never met before. The guy who invited me wasn't even going. To be honest, spending a weekend with men of different denominations, ages, occupations, and stations in life didn't excite me. Making matters worse, we rode to the retreat on a big yellow school bus. I immediately began to wonder, *What have I gotten myself into?!*

As the bus ride got underway, feeling nervous and way out of my comfort zone, I seriously thought about climbing out a window when the bus stopped at a light—until I discovered that the windows only came halfway down. Realizing I had no way out and remembering my commitment to Susy, I remained on the bus and sullenly resolved to gut it out.

At the retreat center, we were directed to a room full of tables. *I'm going to sit here and leave these guys alone,* I thought.

I'm committed to being here, but that's it. So there I sat, drumming my fingers and not saying a word to anyone. To my surprise, the atmosphere changed quickly.

Some men got up and began talking honestly about their lives in terms that were relevant to me. Since they were businessmen like me, they were dealing with some of the same issues I had been facing. The common thread of all these talks was how, after a time of hardship and wondering, their lives had experienced a fundamental change, a dramatic turn for the better that had started when they'd had a personal encounter with Jesus.

I thought back to Paul Johnson's talk. These men had reached some of the same conclusions about life he had. And like Paul Johnson, they each seemed to have discovered a peace that I had never been able to find. They had my attention.

One after another, they affirmed that God knows and loves each one of us personally—so much, in fact, that He actually paid us a visit, coming to earth in the person of Jesus Christ. This Jesus walked the earth as both fully God and fully man, lived a perfect life, and then voluntarily took upon Himself the punishment for all of our guilt and wrongdoing. Every single thing I had ever done wrong in my thoughts, words, and actions had been paid for by Jesus, once and for all through His choice to voluntarily subject Himself to suffering and death on the cross— for me.

The speakers explained that Jesus had died, risen again and appeared to more than 500 witnesses before returning to heaven. By believing in Him as my Lord and receiving Him as my Savior, I could have peace and forgiveness for my sins, and live forever in harmony and in a right relationship with the God who made me. Although these businessmen up front were talking to the entire group, it seemed like each one was speaking to me personally. As these truths sank in, something profound happened inside me.

Knowing God

A couple of weeks after this retreat, a friend again invited me to a CBMC luncheon. This time I eagerly agreed to go. An insurance executive named Art DeMoss told his story of how he was introduced to Christ. By this time, it had a familiar ring to it, and it was exciting to me. As he described what had happened in his life, I realized I had taken a similar step. Interestingly, to this day I can't pinpoint the exact moment when I began a personal relationship with Jesus. I just know it happened. From that time on, my life began to change. I have never been the same since.

At the end of Art's talk, he closed in a prayer and invited guests to pray silently with him if they wanted to invite Christ into their hearts and lives. Although I felt He had already come into my life, I repeated the prayer to reaffirm my commitment. Again I told God how sorry I was for the way I had lived, for the wrong things I had said and done, and for the good things I had failed to do. I asked for His forgiveness and asked for Him to change me.

For the first time in my life, I finally had a place to put my hurt, my pain, and my guilt—at the foot of the cross. Knowing Jesus, I finally had a Friend who would never leave me, a Comforter who could always understand me, a Protector who would never abandon me, and a Heavenly Father who would always love and accept me.

It was quite a process that God used as He began to work in my life. I'll never forget the first time I understood that my sins were forgiven once and for all, not because I'm good (even today I'm still not always good), but because God loves me. Even though it was more than thirty-four years ago, I can still remember feeling that a huge weight had been lifted off my back.

Slowly, things began to improve in my life. I apologized to Susy for my anger, verbal abuse and all the ways I had hurt her. As the weeks and months passed, she watched in stunned amazement as genuine growth began to take place in my life as I found more and more peace and rest through Jesus Christ.

Tragically, I had already destroyed our marriage. But when Susy saw me change, she too decided to accept Jesus Christ as Lord and Savior. With both of us now living in relationship with God, He began rebuilding our marriage from the ground up.

Marriage Broken, Marriage Restored

Today we are madly in love with each other and shudder to think how close we came to losing the love we share. My life is absolutely changed. I can't tell you the amazing difference I feel since meeting Christ.

Sure, I still have my times of tension and remembered pain. Some of those issues took years to work through, which I share about in detail in the next two chapters. But those moments are now few and far between and they no longer have the power over me they once did. I am defined by a whole new sense of peace, contentment, security, and freedom from guilt and fear that I never thought could be possible. And it is possible for you as well.

Maybe you have discovered the futility of trying to find peace and satisfaction in what money can buy, or from entertainment, romance, vacations, work, success, or friends. Maybe you have tried to "get right" with God by attending church and loading yourself down with religious activities and moral obligations while knowing all along that, deep down, something is still missing.

We have included a further discussion of these subjects in Chapter 8. I am grateful that God's invitation to a relationship with Him arrested my attention when it did. It was the beginning of a brand new life for me. Though the next stage of my personal journey wasn't easy, it was a season of growth and healing through which He never left my side as He led me onward toward the kind of life I had always wanted to live.

Questions For Reflectiom

1. What do you feel most: guilt, anger or loneliness?

2. When have you felt guilt-free and full of joy?

3. What is your view of Jesus?

4. Have you "earned" his love or received it without merit?

5. What do you get from God?

6. What do you want from God?

CHAPTER THREE

Finding Healing

No matter what your life has been like, it has no doubt included some measure of pain. Perhaps great pain. Every person has been impacted by the conflicts and wounds that accompany life in a broken world. There is a growing awareness in our day that PTSD is not a condition that only afflicts veterans of battlefield combat. A person who has undergone any kind of life pain may experience many or all of the aspects of this condition.

Your post-traumatic stress may be the result of war, a car accident, the death of someone close to you, a break-up, professional loss, or childhood abuse. Regardless of what you have been through, significant pain of any variety never takes up residence in our lives alone. Life wounds always produce side effects: visible behaviors and private thought patterns that are symptomatic of what is going on inside of us.

What has been your war? How have you been hurt?

In more intimate detail than I ever have before, I would like to share with you the inside story of what my struggle with post-traumatic stress has been like. But more than that, I will also be sharing with you the most helpful, valuable principles I have learned through these years of struggle.

I am delighted to be able to tell you that, no matter how much trauma you have experienced, there are real answers to be found. Relief and freedom are possible. I am stunned at the difference between who I am today, and who I once was.

To be sure, in this life, I doubt anyone ever completely stops having to deal with the fallout of deep wounds. And yet, struggling successfully against these forces in our lives is absolutely possible.

So I eagerly offer you this next portion of my life story. I have presented it by topic as opposed to strict chronological sequence so that I can discuss in greater depth the individual issues I have wrestled with over the years. I hope what I have to share will be of some encouragement and assistance to you, and if nothing else, will remind you that you are not alone.

Guilt

Without question, one of my biggest challenges with post-traumatic stress has been dealing with the powerful and destructive force of guilt. Guilt has been especially hard to keep at bay when I have failed at something related to a relationship or my professional life. Such failure would trigger thoughts like, "If John Atkinson had lived instead of me, surely he would be doing better with his life than I am." I felt pressure to make my life worthwhile and to live up to the standard John had set as a man and a husband.

Although not physically wounded after coming home from the war, my overwhelming sense of guilt made me feel like I was hemorrhaging all the time. Because of this, I cannot begin to describe to you my great relief when I found forgiveness in Christ. It felt like a salve to my heart.

I was amazed that Jesus suffered all that pain and traded in His life for mine simply because He loved me, and that He wanted to give me a life-changing peace for free that I knew I could never earn. Paul explains in Ephesians 2:8-9 "For it is by grace you have been saved, through faith—and this not from yourselves, it is the gift of God—not by works, so that no one can boast." The liberating truth of these verses became the constant meditation of my heart. God's free gift of new life became my most treasured possession.

After spending so many years trying to make up for—or forget—all the mistakes I had made in my past, I realized I was running from something that, horrible as it was, had a solution. I had been living the life of a fugitive for no reason. Yes, like everyone, I was a man who had committed many sins and made many mistakes. As Isaiah 53:6a puts it, "We all, like sheep, have gone astray, each of us has turned to his own way." I knew this problem had divided me from God.

But the wonderful news was that all of my guilt and failures were exactly what Jesus had died to save me from. They didn't surprise Him or shake my standing with Him as His child. I didn't have to try to clean myself up before coming to Him for peace.

As His follower, I could live every day understanding that He had voluntarily taken my place in death and punishment, in spite of knowing all my ugliness and shame, just as John had involuntarily taken my place in death. Knowing Jesus, I could now be free of my sin and leave behind all the guilt and self-condemnation that went with it—for eternity!

Truly, in a world where guilt is so common, there's nothing in the world like having a constant, unchanging source of acceptance and forgiveness from the One who made you.

In John 1:12, we learn that anyone who has received Jesus and believed in Him can have complete confidence that they have been adopted as a child of God. Salvation is an introduction to a new family and a new life. Becoming a believer in Christ really is like being born all over again!

As I began to live beneath the guilt-proof shelter of God's love for me, I must have looked like I was walking ten feet off the ground! I was finally free of the chains of regret and self-loathing that had for so long been wrapped around my heart and soul.

Fear Factor

In addition to guilt, in those years after I returned from Viet Nam I was also haunted by a deep-seated fear and anxiety that I couldn't shake off. It was like it had gotten into my bones. In Viet Nam I had learned that I needed to be constantly on guard from danger just to survive. Being ambushed from every direction without a second's notice and seeing close friends blown to pieces before my eyes taught me to live with a tense readiness.

After coming home, I walked through life suspicious of everyone, tense for attack at any moment. When a perspective on the world is this forcefully built into your mind, it is not easily removed. Taking off my jungle fatigues and dropping my ammo belt didn't magically turn it off.

Wherever I went, I found myself wary of everyone around me, always conscious of my surroundings, scanning where a sniper attack might come from, and where I would take cover if I suddenly started taking incoming fire. To this day, I am constantly aware of people's hands, the briefcases they're carrying, and what position they're in with respect to me.

Despite being stateside, whenever something surprising or threatening would trigger that familiar "fight or flight" reflex, a sudden wave of fear and adrenaline would wash over me and push everything inside me to prepare to fight for my life.

When I would react out of fear and lose my temper with my wife, she would often say to me, "Phil, I'm on your side!" She felt I was acting like I was still at war. And I was. My fears had brought the war home with me.

As much as I tried to control my reflexes, my battle-hardened instincts continued to push me to go on the offensive in everyday situations. Traffic rudeness wasn't just an inconvenience—it was a personal threat that often resulted in shaking my fist and screaming in rage at other drivers. There are a few rent-a-car agents who received my wrath when events didn't go as planned, and there are other people in my life whose dinners I've had to buy to demonstrate my sincere regret for the results of my anger.

I finally found solace and resolution to my fear in recognizing that it was not up to me to overcome or defend myself against the chaos and dangers of this world. I had a sovereign Father, an all-powerful God, who held the waters of the Earth in the palm of His hand with indescribable power. The Living God, who knew everything and was not limited by time and space, cared for me personally.

Philippians 4:6-7 quickly became life verses for me. They read, "Be anxious for nothing, but in everything, by prayer and supplication with thanksgiving let your requests be made known to God. And the peace of God, which surpasses all comprehension, will guard your hearts and your minds in Christ Jesus."

My struggle to overcome fear has not been easy. On a daily basis I have had to saturate my heart, mind, and memories with passages like Isaiah 41:10: "Do not fear, for I am with you; Do not anxiously look about you, for I am your God. I will strengthen you, surely I will help you, Surely I will uphold you with My righteous right hand."

One of my favorite passages on which to meditate is Matthew 6:19-34. No matter what difficult events He might allow in my life, I know that because I am God's child, they are never expressions of His wrath or anger toward me. I can be totally confident in God's constant and unchangeable love. When I am anxious and filled with worry, I am choosing to walk away from these truths and from the God who loves me completely, choosing rather to try to run my life and handle my problems on my own.

When I have found myself once again in those dark places of fear, defensiveness, and self-protective suspicion, I have learned to recognize my anxiety as a signal that I have strayed from resting in the Lord. I have to let Him direct my attention, my thoughts, and my desires back to the promises of His Word which remind me that the only true foundation of peace is in an intimate walk of trust and friendship with Jesus Christ.

The Value of Comfort

The horrors of war I experienced left my mind and memories choked with the sounds of agonizing screams, the smells of burnt flesh, and the thunder of chopper blades roaring above me. All those memories were carved on the inside of my soul. My first step in learning how to deal with my remembered pain was becoming willing to admit to myself and to others that I was hurt in the first place, and that much of my poor conduct resulted from the pain. For some of us, this can be pretty tough to do. We think that admitting we have been hurt is a sign of weakness. But it is actually a sign that we are human.

I learned to ask for comfort from those around me, particularly from my wife. This was a huge breakthrough for me. For many years in our culture, it has been almost unthinkable for a grown man to be vulnerable enough to ask for comfort. We fear this will be seen as weakness, a sign of failure, or a poor reflection on our masculinity.

Female soldiers, surgeons, teachers, office workers, and pilots also often feel pressured to keep up the illusion of self-sufficiency. As men and women, all of us are tempted to bottle up our emotions rather than share them honestly with those close to us. This kind of self-disclosure feels risky. But if we bottle up what we are feeling for long enough, our anxiety and pain will inevitably surface—at the work place, in an addiction, or in family relationships.

For Susy, giving comfort to me was not particularly natural. Her upbringing had been so stable and free of conflict that she had no frame of reference for comforting a fellow adult over wounds that had been inflicted many years before. But as she learned to speak words of love, support, and comfort into the places in my life where I needed them most, she became my most precious and faithful source of understanding and healing on this earth.

In our marriage book, *Unlimited Partnership*, we explain that every person has a cup that represents their emotional capacity. When my positive emotions at the top of the cup were being pushed out by the hurt and pain of my past that filled my cup below, my negative emotions would overflow, taking the form of rage, controlling dominance, or verbal attacks.

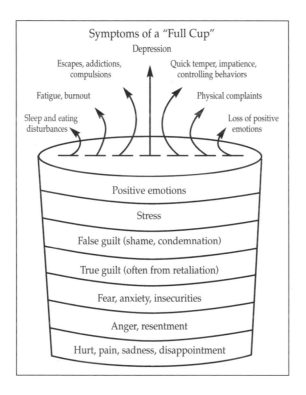

I found that the principles and practices of receiving God's forgiveness and love and trusting Him with all of my heart were effective ways of countering these behaviors. But another core need was to salve the underlying pain through the power of human comfort. I found there were three actions I had to take in order for the destructive power of remembered pain to begin to heal:

1. Admit that I had the pain without using it as an excuse for the wrong attitudes, decisions, and actions that could result from it.

2. Receive comforting words and encouragement from my closest friend and confidant, which for me was my wife, Susy.

3. Go to the Scripture and read, meditate on, and soak in the comforting truths that the God of the Universe holds me up with His victorious right hand, that He commands me to cast my cares on Him, that He has chosen me, that I have a purpose, and that He loves me. The list goes on and on. In the first chapter of Ephesians, I count at least fifteen of these priceless promises. How many can you count? That's the beauty of delving into the Scripture. It is a treasure trove of endless wealth for the human heart.

We explain this in much more depth in Chapter 6 of *Unlimited Partnership.*

Living With Stress

Responding poorly to stress in my life is a challenge that I have largely overcome as I have applied and lived out the principles described above. However, I have some inclinations to stress about certain things in my life that are not going to change.

I will always want to be early, which is my definition of being "on time." When someone disrupts my ability to be early, I am going to feel stressed. One of the solutions for that is being willing to communicate my needs, personality, and personal strengths and weaknesses to those in my family and at work ahead of time in order to avoid some of the moments of tension which would otherwise result.

We all have relational needs that are unique to us. If we are not getting these needs met, then we will experience various kinds of consequences in our lives, such as frustration, loneliness, or stress. I have been able to discuss this subject with others by showing them the Intimacy Needs Inventory. The inventory lists the top intimacy needs that people most commonly have, including their definitions.

Here is a list of ten key intimacy needs and biblical references which encourage our selfless giving to one another:

- **Acceptance** - Deliberate and ready reception with a favorable response; to receive willingly; to regard as good and proper. *"Wherefore accept one another, just as Christ also accepted us to the glory of God"* (Romans 15:7).

- **Affection** - To communicate care and closeness through physical touch and affirming words. *"Greet one another with a holy kiss"* (Romans 16:16).

- **Appreciation** - To recognize with gratitude; to communicate with words and feelings personal gratefulness for another person; to praise. *"I praise you . . ."* (1 Corinthians 11:2).

- **Approval** - To accept as satisfactory; to give formal or official sanction to; to have or express a favorable opinion; to approve of. *"Because anyone who serves Christ in this way is pleasing to God and approved by men"* (Romans 14:18).

- **Attention** - To take thought of another and convey appropriate interest, concern, and support; to enter into another's world. *"But that the members (of the body) should have the same care for one another"* (1 Corinthians 12:25).

- **Comfort** - To give strength and hope to; to ease grief or trouble; to console, cheer. *"The God of all comfort, who comforts us in all our troubles, so that we can comfort those in any trouble"* (2 Corinthians 1:3,4).

- **Encouragement** - To urge forward and positively persuade toward a goal; to inspire with courage, spirit, or hope; to stimulate. *"Therefore encourage one another and build each other up"* (1 Thessalonians 5:11).

- **Respect** - To value and regard highly; to convey great worth; to esteem. *"Show proper respect to everyone"* (1 Peter 2:17).

- **Security** - Freedom from exposure to danger; to put beyond hazard of losing, want, or deprivation; confidence of "harmony" in relationships. *"May those who love You be secure"* (Psalm 122:6).

- **Support/Bear Burden** - To come alongside and gently help carry a burden; to assist in a struggle or problem; to provide for. *"Carry each other's burdens, and in this way you will fulfill the law of Christ"* (Galatians 6:2).

The most effective way to use this tool is to first pause and reflect on which three needs you might most enjoy receiving from your spouse or someone else close to you, and then guess which three he or she might most enjoy receiving from you. Ask that person to score you on how you are doing in fulfilling their needs on a scale of 1-10 (with 1 being poor and 10 being excellent). Then ask them what their top three intimacy needs are—and most importantly, what it looks like to them to have those needs fulfilled.

For example, two people may both have a high need for respect but experience or receive it in two very different ways. For one person it may mean listening to his or her opinion and for another it may mean showing up on time for an appointment.

For many people the need for security might primarily concern finances. For Susy, however, it is more related to emotional safety. She needs to feel confident that I won't randomly explode in anger at her when I am having a Viet Nam flashback. Talking through these needs and how they can practically be met in our lives can go a long way to decreasing the relational conflicts and points of stress that can so often be a part of daily life.

As I had these conversations with more and more people in my life, we began not only to understand each other much better, but also to love each other better. Soon family, friends, and co-workers began to see a real change in my life as our relationships began growing in strength and closeness. Soon they were the ones in various situations asking me how I was doing and how they could help.

Living with this level of openness took more courage and confidence than I had at times. But as I continued to practice vulnerable honesty, I grew in my trust for people even as they grew in their ability to understand and relate to me.

I shared with Susy my need for her affection and physical touch and she learned to grow in tenderness toward me. When she simply touches my hand in a loving way or rubs my neck, I actually feel the pain, stress, and pressure drain out of me. I also communicated to her my high need for verbal encouragement.

I have many negative messages that run through my mind, such as, "You're no good," "You're always going to be a failure," "John is dead," "You guys lost the war," "You're just a baby killer," "You're a disgrace," "You're fired." As these phrases echo through my head, they scream pain and stress to me. But Susy's faithfulness to give me verbal encouragement replaces those old damaging thoughts with the present reality of her love, acceptance and approval. In times when those voices are especially loud in my head, Susy will sit and read Scripture to me, replacing the lies in my mind with the truth of God's love and faithfulness toward me.

Some would say I am trying to get from my wife what I should seek only from God. But Susy is one of God's greatest means of helping me experience His love for me. She is a vessel of His love in my life, a picture of His heart. God wants to recruit all of us to become comforters in each other's lives.

If there is someone close to you who might be willing to step into this kind of role in your life, I would encourage you to have the boldness and vulnerability to admit what a blessing it would be to receive comfort from such a close friend. You may be pleasantly surprised at their response. Just as when someone has been hunting for the perfect birthday present for a treasured friend, perhaps they have been searching for a long time for a way to offer something that will really be meaningful to you. This may be just the invitation they have been waiting for.

Anger and Rage

It is true that anger is a natural emotion. But most of the time what we do with it is sinful and destructive. James 1:20 says that "The anger of man does not achieve the righteousness of God." Ephesians 4:26 warns that you should not allow the sun to go down on your anger.

When you go to sleep stewing about something that made you mad, you "give the devil a foothold" in your life (verse 27). In other words, you wake up the next morning and you have a greater enemy than you had the night before. The enemy has now gotten inside the walls of your life through the Trojan Horse of your own anger.

That's when you can turn into what the wife of a friend of mine calls the Impostor. When her husband gets irritable and starts to vent his anger, his wife says lightheartedly, "Uh oh, the Impostor has shown up!" She means that he is not living as if he is forgiven and loved by God, but rather has returned to the old life he once lived before meeting Christ. Her good humored reminders have served to help my friend, who is a giant of a man in character and competency, turn back to living out the truth that God has called us "out of darkness into His marvelous light" (1 Peter 2:9).

When the Impostor shows up in my life, I have to humble myself and admit that I am letting myself be controlled by anger and rage, rather than the fruits of the Spirit. My goal is to let my choices, attitudes, and words form out of the love, joy, peace, patience, kindness, goodness, gentleness, faithfulness and self control that result when I daily yield my life to Jesus Christ (Galatians 5:22).

A friend of mine told me once that when I am stressed, it is usually a sign that I am in sin. The most common reason I am stressed is that I have taken ownership and control of my circumstances instead of remembering that the Lord is in control. He holds every one of the moments of our lives in His hand. It is not our job to figure out every detail or perfectly prepare for the future. Our job is to do our best and trust the Lord with the outcome.

New Every Morning

One of the times in my day that the Impostor uses to get a grip on me is when my alarm goes off and I decide to hit the snooze button. I believe that snoozing and tossing and turning in bed is often the devil's playground. It is for me, at least. When our minds are in that half-asleep state, we are not in control of what enters our heads. We are more vulnerable to thinking angry, fearful, lustful, or guilt-ridden thoughts.

Because the dreams that a person remembers are usually the ones that come just before waking, snoozing dramatically increases the number of dreams a person remembers in the morning. For people like me who have experienced a large number of difficult events in life, snoozing is a very negative way to begin the day. That's why I set my alarm and do my best to get up the first time it goes off. Even though it might feel better to sleep in and put off starting my day, this practice can put me on the wrong side of more than just my schedule.

I have learned that the way we structure our morning routines is strategically very important not only for each individual day, but also for the ultimate direction of our lives. As a human being, my natural inclination is to forget that God has chosen me, forgiven me, and is changing me into a man of peace rather than someone driven by an inner war. So I have a great need to reconnect with Him and the promises He has given me before other circumstances rush in to steal my attention and focus. I do this on a daily basis in what I call my Quiet Time.

Early in the morning before anyone else is awake, I pour out my heart to the Lord. I tell Him what I'm feeling, what I'm thinking, and what I'm worrying about—everything I want to leave with Him. Then I let Him pour into my heart and mind the truths of His promises and character from His Word. Sometimes I read Scripture verses that I haven't read yet that year. Some passages I have read literally hundreds of times as God bathes my soul in the promises of His Word that most perfectly fit the needs I have in my life.

I remember when I had to take a blood pressure medicine as well as a beta blocker to help my heart function properly after my heart surgery. I did this faithfully every morning and every night, knowing that this was best for me. Similarly, there are some verses that I go back to over and over again to recall to my mind and retrain my heart on how to handle my pain, anger, and fear.

I want to be able to live as the Apostle Paul did. He learned to be content in whatever circumstances he was in—whether he was enjoying comfort and prosperity or experiencing great need and hardship (Phil 4:11-12). I want to be so conscious of the faithfulness and love of God that I can live with a heart filled with contentment in every circumstance. My Quiet Time in the morning is when God deepens and grows this kind of life in me.

Some days, my Quiet Times have had to begin before I have even put my feet on the floor. There have been some mornings when I have felt so much discouragement and pain that I have not even been able to get out of bed until I have been washed in the peace and security of repeating the truths of God's love and faithfulness. I have actually had to worship and pray out loud until I am able to feel what I know.

Some people play worship music in order to let the truth and beauty of God fill their minds. My approach is to sing truth because it gets me involved. Singing "Hallelujah" and worshiping God aloud is a great release and ministry to my soul and helps silence the voices from my past. I love the simple praise choruses that draw my heart to the person of Jesus Christ, such as: "He is Lord, He is Lord. He is risen from the dead and He is Lord. Every knee shall bow, every tongue confess that Jesus Christ is Lord."

I keep it up until it begins to sink in that, because of God's love, I am more than a conqueror, I am a chosen child of His, I have been adopted by the King, I am the friend of God, Jesus has forgiven me, I am utterly loved, I will live with Him forever, He cares for me, and He has healed me. For a person with a crushed heart, singing softly for fifteen minutes or even thirty minutes may be just the right way for the love of God to fill up their thoughts and emotions at the start of the day.

On more typical days, I begin my Quiet Time with three lists. At the top of a sheet of paper I write out 1 John 1:9, which says, "If we confess our sins, he is faithful and just and will forgive our sins and purify us from all unrighteousness." I then write down what I need to confess: my selfishness, my harsh words, my wrong thoughts, my unloving actions—whatever they might be.

Then I consciously embrace with joy the mercy and the forgiveness of God. This practice enables me to live with something that is precious and rare in our world—a clear conscience! I believe that much of the weight of darkness that so many people live under everyday is due to ignoring this valuable gift and the simple path to obtaining it.

Second, I write down Proverbs 3:5-6, which says, "Trust in the Lord with all your heart and lean not on your own understanding. In all your ways acknowledge Him, and He will direct your paths." I write every issue I am worried about, the fears that keep me awake at night, and the anxieties that crowd into my thoughts during the day. I consciously give each of these to God and choose to receive His peace. In giving my burdens to God, I am choosing to receive the peace that comes from knowing that my God is good, loving, and worthy of my trust.

Third, I make a list of what I need to be doing. Often God gives me the most wonderful ideas about problems I don't know how to solve or responsibilities I had forgotten. I don't think it's a coincidence that He often puts these thoughts and insights in my mind after I have submitted to Him all my guilt, pain, fears, and sin to be covered by His grace, healing, security, and love. When my mind is freed from the stranglehold of all these negative thoughts, I am far more free to hear from and follow the guidance of my Heavenly Father.

I keep these three lists on my heart, on my computer, or on a piece of paper as I proceed with the rest of my Quiet Time. This time consists of prayer and really soaking my mind in the passages of Scripture that I am reading that day. It is incredible the difference it makes to begin my day this way.

Life in our culture and time tends to contribute urgency, complexity, noise, and a sense of crisis to our daily lives. These times in the morning when I am able to calm my soul and bring it into the stillness and companionship of the Living God, enable me to weather the storms of my day anchored by the Rock of Ages. His Word is life and spiritual food to me—to all of us. On good or on difficult mornings, my time with God drains the oldness out of me and puts into me what is new. Lamentations 3:19-26 puts it beautifully:

> I remember my affliction and my wandering,
> the bitterness and the gall.
> I well remember them,
> and my soul is downcast within me.
> Yet this I call to mind
> and therefore I have hope:

Because of the Lord's great love we are not consumed,

for His compassions never fail.

They are new every morning;

great is Your faithfulness.

I say to myself, "The Lord is my portion;

therefore I will wait for Him."

The Lord is good to those whose hope is in Him,

to the one who seeks Him;

it is good to wait quietly

for the salvation of the Lord.

The Forward Lean

After my Quiet Time, if I am doing well, I try to do the difficult items first. I say to myself, "I am not leaving my office until I have the hard stuff completely done." There is great value in kicking the habit of putting off doing what is in front of you just because it is intimidating. Weeks, months, years, careers, families, and legacies have been flushed down the drain by the words, "I will get to that later." There is no later! The present moment is the only time life can be lived. Tomorrow, this moment will already be gone forever. The question is, what should you be doing right now? What are you putting off? Freedom, courage, and fruitfulness are never the products of procrastination.

Though I do my best not to put off the challenges, there are days when I am frankly not at my best. On these days, applying the forward lean requires a less severe angle. If I am struggling with discouragement or depression, I cannot simply charge ahead and take on the most difficult task in front of me first thing in the morning. To get it done at all that day, I need to be more strategic. Like a winding road that gently climbs a mountain, I avoid attempting to accomplish more than I can immediately handle, while still planning to get that hard stuff done by the end of the day.

With this strategy in mind, I find one easy task to do and I start there. I pick something simple, like resetting my watch or my clock, and then I move on to what is next on the list. If I am behind on my jogging and discouraged about it, I make the decision to walk for 10 minutes. Anybody can walk for 10 minutes, right? If I get out every day and walk for 10 minutes, it's not long before I find myself walking for 40 minutes or jogging for 20 minutes. Or 30 minutes.

I know that I need to work out to stay healthy, so I start out doing just a couple of push-ups and sit-ups at a time. But, I do them every day. Some mornings I wake up and I just hate doing them. On those days I tell myself, "I'm just going to do one." If you just do one push-up every day, pretty soon, you'll be up to 3 and then 6, 12, 18 and so forth.

For me, the key on tough days is to start somewhere and refuse to quit. When you're discouraged, moving forward requires taking a few small steps at a time. The key isn't how big the step is, only that you take one—and that you take another one and never quit moving forward.

I have also found that part of living with a forward lean involves working toward excellence in the details of life. There are many specific things I have learned over the years that have been helpful to me on a practical level. Here are a few of them:

- Live on a budget. There is great freedom in not having people call you about bills.

- Spend time with godly people who are fun, loving, and encouraging.

- Stay connected to a strong, vibrant local church that will nourish you relationally and spiritually.

- Read a Psalm before going to sleep at night. This makes the last words on your mind the promises of God and the prayers of a faithful man like King David.

- Stay up-to-date with close friends to whom you can be accountable on your weaknesses and temptations. This will help keep you from waking up one day to realize that you have strayed into sins and destructive patterns of behavior that you mistakenly thought you could handle on your own.

- Look for people and organizations whose work you believe in and which you can support financially.

- Find ways to use and develop your gifts and abilities.

- Staff your weaknesses by depending on the teamwork of others.

- Spend regular, unhurried time with your wife and children.

- Spend more time reading books than watching TV or movies.

- Carry a pen and 3x5 card in your pocket for writing down ideas.

None of these practices will make or break my day or my year. But I have learned that sometimes moving forward is largely about collecting small victories over time until, piece by piece, goals begin falling into place.

Time-Outs

Susy and I have found that taking time-outs has been a useful technique in dealing with my poor reactions to difficult situations. When I realize that I am being impatient or harsh, Susy or I will say, "I need a few minutes." We then go to a separate place for 5 or 10 minutes to pray. I pray for God's encouragement, strength and wisdom and she prays that I would have God's patience.

After praying separately, we come back together again and if she can tell I need it, Susy expresses some words of encouragement, understanding, and support. She will say something like, "Phil, you are doing great. You're an outstanding dad. You're a wonderful husband. You work so hard. You care so much for all of us and provide well for our family." If she runs out of what to say after six or seven comments, sometimes I ask her to say them again.

Those words of affirmation and love replace the loop of negative thoughts that can be playing in my mind. Sometimes we have had to repeat this process a few times. But in the end, this has been a very effective way for us to avert relational collisions when my emotional cup has been full and about to spill over.

If you think about it, taking time-outs is a very common-sense idea. When a quarterback gets disoriented about what to do or makes a few mistakes in a row, it is common practice for him to call a time-out for the team to regroup, get a breather, and review the game plan. Then they return to the field ready to get back in the game.

I do the same thing. Within a few minutes I start to regain God's perspective on myself and my world. Then I'm ready to get back to the matter at hand, whether it is a financial challenge, an item of business, or a people problem. Time-outs give me the margin to work through my emotions and mistakes in a way that is beneficial, rather than hurtful, to myself and others.

For years, I used to react instinctively when I felt strong emotions rising. Now I have learned to respond in a more measured, self-controlled way that allows me to work through what I am feeling and also enables those around me to be a part of the process as well.

Healthy Emoting

Have you ever thought about how much a paper cut hurts? You may weigh 130 or 230 pounds. You may be 18 or 88. You may be a weightlifter, a fighter pilot, a machine gunner, a machinist, a business executive, or a doctor. You may have diplomas and awards on the wall. But regardless of any of this, when you get a paper cut, it hurts! And this tiny little paper cut that you can barely see hurts for days. Depending on where it is, it can change the way you turn your car key in the ignition and the way you open your wallet to dig for a five dollar bill. For a few days, a little paper cut can change your life.

Imagine now with me the impact of a much greater kind of pain. Whether your wounds have come from losing a child, a marriage, a battle, or a best friend, that trauma has left its mark on your heart and on the way you live your life. If those of us who have received such scars will be willing to admit the pain and to receive comfort and encouragement, we will not only find ourselves on the path to healing, but we will also become capable of leading others in that direction as well.

A study was done by the American Bar Association that surveyed what clients want most from their lawyer. You would probably think they want someone who is ruthless, well-educated, fiercely persistent, and will strive to win at all costs. The ABA study found, however, the top thing clients want from their lawyer is somebody who cares about them and their case.

If this is true of legal representatives, how much more is it true that we expect a doctor to care about us, or a mentor, a best friend, a husband, or wife? Care and empathy deeply touch the human soul. In a world where difficulty and hurt are a part of life, receiving the caring love of others is vital to our emotional health.

When Jesus Christ came to earth, He walked from village to town to city caring for those who were sick, maimed, downcast, and rejected. He cared so much for us that He gave His life on the cross for everything we've done, past, present, and future. By receiving His love, His forgiveness, and His free gift of eternal life, we too can become vessels of His compassion and empathy for others.

2 Corinthians 1:3-4 says that our Lord is the "God of all comfort; who comforts us in all our affliction so that we may be able to comfort those who are in any affliction with the comfort

with which we ourselves are comforted by God." Receiving the comfort of God for us, and passing it along to those around us, is one of the most meaningful and impacting ways a person can live his or her life.

Once we have acknowledged and have begun to overcome our own struggles, we are able to become a refuge for others who are still living under the full load of what they have experienced. Through our willingness to admit and understand our pain and to receive comfort from God and others, we now can be understanding and empathetic to those God brings across our path.

This is a powerful principle for relationships whether you are a father, husband, wife, mother, teacher, pastor, or lawyer. People who genuinely care about others are the ones that executives want to hire to handle their problems and to whom friends want to go in times of need. As Matthew 5:5 says, "Blessed are the gentle, for they shall inherit the earth." When we value people and are concerned about their needs rather than focusing on our own goals, we are able to experience what life and relationships were meant to be.

Questions For Reflection

1. How often would you say that you feel isolated or misunderstood?

2. How many times per week are you filled with stress? Fear? Anger? Guilt?

3. Why do you think so many of us do not open up to others about hard or hurtful experiences from our past?

4. Do you think you are more likely to grow through the wounds of your past on your own or in the company of one or more people, whom you feel truly understand and support you? Why?

5. Have you ever openly shared with someone close to you about

the experiences of your past, including the difficult ones? If so, how did they respond?

6. If those around you knew how they could help and encourage you in your life, do you think they would?

7. Who are the top two or three people you know with whom you would feel most comfortable opening up?

CHAPTER FOUR

Life Beyond the Scars

Working through the fallout of trauma is never an easy process. Over time, however, I began to feel like I was making significant progress. I was learning how to identify and express the emotions I was feeling, and do so in a healthy way that didn't compound my own pain by hurting others. I was finally getting a grip on how to escape the undertow of the overwhelming guilt and fear that would so often wash over me.

Through the strength of God and the faithful love of my wife, Susy, I also saw my anger decrease over time. But just when I thought I should be reaching the end of this process of healing, I realized that I was only part way through dealing with the pain of my past. It turns out, healing from our wounds is only half the story. Even after healing is significantly underway, we still have to work through the scars.

Scars are caused by wounds, but they still remain even after those wounds have been partially or fully healed. Scars are the residual effects of past trauma that are apparent in your current life despite the comfort, understanding, and love you have experienced since. One might think that because my battles with anger, fear, guilt, and aggression were caused by experiencing pain, healing this pain would completely remove these struggles. But this is not the case. Beyond the pain they cause, wounds leave a person marked, inscribed with a cruel signature that, if allowed, can hover over a person with maiming force for the rest of his or her life.

Determined this would not be my fate, I began working on taking not only my pain to God, but also those aspects of my attitudes, habits, and ways of thinking which were still disfigured by the scar tissue of old wounds. In addition to asking God for healing, I began to ask Him to initiate a kind of physical therapy in my life and heart.

I knew there were many ways in which I was walking through life with a deep soul-weariness and a limp. Thankfully, there is life to be found beyond the scars. God answered my prayer, and soon began to teach me all over again what it means to walk with Him in His power, thinking and living as I was always designed to. It did not happen overnight, but eventually I began to experience God's gifts of strength and wholeness described in Isaiah 40:28-31:

Do you not know? Have you not heard?

The Lord is the everlasting God,

The Creator of the ends of the earth.

He will not grow tired or weary,

And His understanding no one can fathom.

He gives strength to the weary

And increases the power of the weak.

Even youths grow tired and weary,

And young men stumble and fall;

But those who hope in the Lord

Will renew their strength.

They will soar on wings like eagles;

They will run and not grow weary,

They will walk and not be faint.

Fighting Flashbacks

Without question, the first area of significant scarring that I had to confront was in my mind. The most difficult aspect of recovering from PTSD for me has been the brutal scenes of war that haunt my mind. I can still vividly remember the screams of broken men as we loaded them onto helicopters, the stench of war, and the cries of wounded and dying men scattered across broken battlefields. Sometimes these events seem as fresh in my mind as the day they took place.

Although I live every day with these memories stored in the back of my mind, sometimes an event will trigger an especially strong flashback and take me right back to those blood-soaked rice paddies. I have had more nights than I care to recall, in which the blackness around me served as a theater of remembered horrors, culminating with me waking up in a cold sweat to the sound of terrified screams—only to realize they were my own.

Whether or not your painful memories are this severe, they are still powerful for you. You may be wondering, as I did for so long, if there is any way to get rid of them or loosen the grip they have on your mind. God has been teaching me to stand firmly against the darkness of my past experiences. As Philippians 4:8 says, "Finally, brethren, whatever is true, whatever is honorable, whatever is right, whatever is pure, whatever is lovely, whatever is of good repute, if there is any excellence and if anything worthy of praise, dwell on these things."

I have learned to apply this verse in a practical way by visually replacing the pictures in my mind that bring trauma, pain, and fear with other images. I have worked to picture Jesus on the cross, dying for me, as opposed to the automatic weapon fire taking out my buddies beside me. When I think of the blood they spilled, I try to think about the blood of Jesus Christ that He willingly shed for me. This helps me move from a graphic image of pain and guilt to one of love.

Over time, when those old images of carnage and loss have stung my mind, I have been able to transfer my focus to the heroic, sacrificial death of Jesus more and more quickly. This has helped me replace my feelings of pain and guilt with a sense of gratefulness and being loved.

The Weapon of the Word

I also memorized verses of Scripture which I carried with me on 3x5 cards, in order to form the habit of meditating on comforting words of truth, rather than on traumatic memories. Romans 12:1 says, "And do not be conformed to this world, but be transformed by the renewing of your mind." Memorizing and meditating on Scripture brings to our minds God's nature, comfort, truth, wisdom, promises, and God's love, crowding and pushing back whatever dark and threatening memories haunt us.

2 Corinthians 10:5 admonishes us to take "every thought captive to the obedience of Christ." Memorizing verses of Scripture arrests those thoughts that do nothing more than burn and pillage my peace of mind. Scripture helps wash my thoughts clean, reminding me that the gracious God of the universe will never leave me or forsake me (Joshua 1:5).

Going Back To Move Forward

To my great surprise, I recently found joy and healing in going back to the very places where so many good men died. As I walked through the towns and fields of Viet Nam, instead of hearing the concussion of bombs and the snapping of bullets flying by, I heard the laughter of children and the cheery voices of men and women shopping for fruit in the local markets. Instead of bombed-out tree lines and fields pock-marked with bomb craters, I saw all around me cascading scenes of lush countryside, showing me for the first time that Viet Nam is beautiful.

Going back to those old places was healing for me. I saw that the rice paddies didn't have to be a threat, and that the noise over a rise in the road could be a village of happy people with farmers working and children at play.

If there are places or relationships in your past that seem like strongholds of dread to you, perhaps the passing years have superficially added to the fear surrounding them in your mind. Like an adult who goes back to a childhood home and is surprised at how much smaller it seems, there are times when returning to visit the events or places that haunt us can reveal to us how much we have grown and how much has changed.

Opening Up

It has also been helpful to me to revisit places and memories through talking about them with people close to me. Over all the years during which people didn't ask me questions, I assumed the worst. I automatically thought they were condemning me, calling me a baby killer under their breath, or making fun of the fact that we were the ones responsible for the only war that America ever lost.

Eventually, however, I realized that people didn't bring up the war because they didn't know what to say. When they finally figured out that I wanted to talk about it, they let me. My kids learned to ask non-threatening questions and just listen, giving value to what I had been through and validating the pain I still felt as I recounted what had happened.

As I shared some of these conversations with my family and close friends, I began to notice I felt closer to them. I felt a greater sense of intimacy—less alone, less misunderstood. I felt like the demons of my past weren't as powerful or as unspeakable as they had been, and that prompted me to venture more into the world of building trusting, open relationships with those around me.

Over the past few decades, I have also consistently looked for opportunities to share my story and how I began a personal relationship with Jesus Christ. I have discovered that every time I talk about Viet Nam or how God rebuilt our marriage after I had destroyed it, I find healing in how it encourages other people.

Often people come up and say that something I shared meant a lot to them, or that their marriage has been improved or brought back from the brink, by the way God has used my story in their lives. These positive events add meaning and positive associations to my old memories, covering them over with the knowledge that God truly does heal lives and bring peace, hope, and love to anyone willing to receive Him.

Honoring Your Limits

There is a practical side to dealing with past trauma. There are some places that I don't go. Returning to the peaceful villages and towns of Viet Nam was a positive experience for me. But I don't like fireworks. I had to walk out of the Gettysburg light and sound diorama. I don't rent vivid, realistic movies that are related to infantry combat or the Viet Nam war. There are some things I am not willing to do, and I don't think that is a sign of weakness. I think it is practical for me to recognize that, because of the war, there are some actions or events that will have a positive effect on my mind and life and some that will not.

Why pointlessly relive something that has brought me so much pain and hurt? With a few exceptions, most of the people who enjoy seeing gruesome war movies are those who have never been to war. There was a time when I was embarrassed to honor these boundaries in my life. But I have since learned a very helpful truth: it is a sign of wisdom, not cowardice, to avoid that which will only drag you down.

Exposing The Lies

Trauma does not only leave emotional scars, however. It can leave our ways of thinking and our belief systems marred as well. That is why we have to learn to expose the lies we have come to believe and understand that can drag down our attitudes and rot our lives from the inside out.

One common lie is that it is acceptable to intimidate others to get what we want. This idea assumes that we are sovereign over our own fates and that we can use others as pawns. It is an attitude that assumes there is no God to provide for our needs or judge our actions. Matthew 5:9 says, "Blessed are the peacemakers, for they shall be called sons of God." As God's children, we are called to use our abilities and influence as avenues of peace, not as forces of manipulation. Truly, the life of the peacemaker is the blessed, happy life.

It is also tempting to say to ourselves, "I am a victim, so I deserve to be given special treatment." If we have a relationship with Christ and have been rescued and freed by Him, however, we aren't victims. We have been saved, given a new name, and adopted into His family. We have a brand new identity, heritage, and destiny. It is this incredible news of our spiritual adoption that makes the Apostle John exclaim, "How great is the love the Father has lavished on us, that we should be called children of God!" (1 John 3:1) Truly, nothing can separate us from the constancy of our heavenly Father's love.

As I have faced the ugliness of my struggles over the years, there have been times I have thought to myself, "Phil, you're just sick! You're a wreck that should be junked." I certainly have wrestled with many problems in my life. But the truth is that I don't have to let my problems define who I am. And neither do you. The key to overcoming them and living in freedom is remembering who I am in Christ. Psalm 139 says that we are fearfully and wonderfully made. Our sovereign God may have allowed some pretty difficult events in our lives. But they do not define us in His eyes, and they should not define us in our own.

If there are times you feel God doesn't care about you because of the terrible circumstances that have happened in your
life, consider this: Jesus proved on the cross, in the most personal way possible, just how much He understands and can relate to
our pain. He suffered and sacrificed His life out of love for us,
declaring to you and me across all these centuries that He would
literally rather die than live without us.

Jesus came to earth, became a man, and took upon Himself
all our sorrows and grief, so we would know that we don't suffer alone. Not only does Jesus suffer with us, He cares so much
for us that He also invites us to throw all our cares onto Him (1
Peter 5:7). When I am tempted to let lies rule my mind and control my attitudes and perspectives, I remember all that Christ
has done to enable me to live in His ways and I pray that I can
accomplish that in His strength.

Aggression vs. Boldness

Before I went to war, I was an undisciplined, promiscuous,
aimless, procrastinating teenager. I was like those described in
Jeremiah 47 who ran from that which was threatening or intimidating, rather than face it. Jeremiah 47:3 says, "Because of
the noise of the galloping hoofs of his stallions, the tumult of
his chariots, and the rumbling of his wheels, the fathers have not
turned back for their children, because of the limpness of their
hands."

The fathers, hearing the rumbling of the pounding hooves of
the horse-drawn chariots, turned and ran, leaving their children
behind, probably along with their wives and other family members. The stronger fathers ran and left behind the people who
were closest to them even though they were the very ones they
were supposed to protect. They ran because they were afraid,
because they were undisciplined, because they wanted the easy
way out—like me as a teenager.

After Viet Nam, I came home a changed man in many ways,
including a newly acquired aggressiveness. My Marine Corps

training and intense combat experience had given me an edge over civilians they didn't even know about. I now had the ability to grit my teeth and accomplish almost anything I set my mind to.

When I went back to college, hitting the books wasn't nearly as hard as it had been before. When I set my sights on going to law school, I decided I was going to do whatever it took to improve my grades and LSAT scores until I got into the school of my choice, and I did.

I would sit in the chair and work until I was finished. It didn't matter what time it was. It didn't matter if I had eaten that day. It didn't matter if I missed a social event. I had learned in the Marine Corps that there can be a high price for slacking off and taking short cuts. I had determined that I was never going to live that way again. I was going to aim for high goals and achieve them no matter what. And that's what I did. But in the meantime, my aggressive no-holds-barred approach to life was beginning to cost me in a different way. And the price was high.

During those early years, I had not yet learned how to avoid living out of fear, guilt, anger, or pain. As a result, though my aggression was helping me climb the social and corporate ladder to success, it was also having a poisonous effect on my life. It caused me to destroy the one relationship that I cared about most—my marriage with, Susy. I hurt the feelings of the people closest to me and got into disagreements and arguments on a regular basis, causing me to have to apologize to many people.

But over the years, as I did my part to apply the principles I have been sharing in this chapter, God tempered and reshaped my aggressiveness into a gentle boldness that has enabled me to pursue excellence without running over people in the process. Romans 8:37 says that we are "more than conquerors through Him who loved us." It is only through the love of Christ that we can truly live as conquerors without becoming conquered by our own drivenness. As this truth began to sink into my life, my approach to pursuing my goals changed.

As an attorney, when I first began to learn how to turn my aggressiveness into a godly, self-controlled boldness, it gave me the ability to handle intimidating situations in court that could have become volatile. I often argued cases in front of judges who were exhausted, frustrated and testy after a long string of tedious trials.

More than once, when a judge would chew me out, my boldness enabled me to listen to him and calmly approach the bench and tell him face-to-face, "Judge, respectfully, I would like to ask to be allowed to finish presenting my evidence. My client's company, reputation, and livelihood are on the line." Because of my demeanor, this direct approach was well received most of the time. When others might have been too stressed or angry to confront this kind of situation with humility and courage, the steady strength that God was growing in my life paid off.

After fifteen years of law practice, God called me into a ministry in which I became heavily involved in mentoring, discipleship, and speaking around the nation. There have been times when I have asked people if they would be willing to consider making a donation to the ministry and they have all but thrown me out of their office. People have made frustrated comments like "Everybody's begging for money these days," and "Why don't you go get a real job?" as a friend once told me. Another time a man said, "Don't tell me about all the troubles at your office and the staff you've had to let go—I have my own problems!"

Years ago, these encounters would have sent me into a rage—at least on the inside. Or they would have made me quit or get depressed. But because I have learned to deal with the stress, anger, guilt, and fear from my combat trauma in a healthy way, words didn't ignite anger or discouragement in me. These experiences simply gave me insight into my friends' lives and helped me understand them better as I continued to persevere in doing my job, including the parts that required courage.

When I was the target of a verbal lashing, I learned to have the boldness to resist the temptation to walk out the door and, instead, to stay put and wait patiently for my friend to calm down. Within a few minutes, he usually was in a frame of mind to explain what else he had to say, which helped me understand where his anger was coming from.

At times, I have spent several hours listening to and comforting my friends and business associates after such outbursts. I have been able to do this because I understood the source of their pain. Because of all the times I had spent trying to understand the sources of my own anger, I knew what to look for. I had a roadmap to their life because I had traveled the same streets of pain. I was therefore able to pass on to them the truths and principles of Scripture that had helped me.

During some of these impromptu meetings, as well as during the ones that followed, significant issues would surface related to depression, marital infidelity, thoughts of suicide or addictive behaviors. Many conversations have led to relationships of ongoing mentoring and discipleship.

As long as my heart and emotions are grounded in God's love for me, my "go for it" approach to life has been a valuable asset in a world that is brimming with obstacles and opportunities. Learning from the hardest experiences in our lives can give us tremendous insight into the human heart. As you work through the challenges in your life over time, you will gain an inner strength that will become a source of solace not only for you, but also for others.

Study nearly any gifted leader, whether King David, the Apostle Paul, Abraham Lincoln, or Winston Churchill, and you will find that their greatness was in large part a product of the character they built as they wrestled with the tremendous obstacles they experienced in life, such as loneliness, persecution, failure, betrayal, broken family relationships, depression, and physical impairment.

The character and boldness they developed as a result of having to overcome so much personal opposition is much of what God used in their lives to prepare them for the unique work He had created them to do. Once you allow God to begin to tame and heal the pain and distrust that lies beneath your aggressiveness, the refined boldness that remains will become a valuable ally to you for effective living in a world hungry for strong leadership.

King Jehoshaphat

I learned in the Marine Corps that Marines don't leave men behind. Marines don't quit. Marines don't run. If we are going to break through whatever struggles we are facing, we are going to have to live with this kind of determination. Perhaps this is why I identify so much with the story of King Jehoshaphat in 2 Chronicles 20. This story contains principles that are applicable and effective in a host of circumstances in our time.

If you have a Bible, I encourage you to open it up to 2 Chronicles chapter 20. As you follow along, feel free to underline the parts of this story that stand out to you. In the first two verses of the chapter, we read that armies from three nations have come from across the sea to wage war against Jehoshaphat and his people. Let's take a look at what Jehoshaphat did in response.

1. Although Jehoshaphat was afraid, he turned his attention to the Lord and did not run (verse 3).

2. He reviewed God's character in order to reaffirm in his heart that our Lord rules over all with power and might so that no one can stand against Him (verse 6).

3. He reviewed what God had already done in driving out a previous enemy (verse 7).

4. He refused to quit and committed to stand fast, saying, "We will stand" (verse 9).

5. He humbled himself, admitting that he was "powerless" and

"did not know what to do." But then he also said out of a heart of faith, "Our eyes are on You" (verse 12).

6. He embraced the truth that the responsibility for the outcome of the battle was not in his hands, but in the Lord's, saying, "Do not be afraid. . .the battle is not yours, but God's. . . ." (verse 15).

7. Jehoshaphat embraced and led others to embrace God's instruction not to fear. Then he and the people under his care did their part by going out to face the enemy, knowing that the Lord was with them (verse 17).

8. In the midst of all of these pressures and dangers, he faithfully worshipped the Lord, bowing his head in humility before the God of all peace, as a man acknowledging that God is greater than the fears he was facing (verse 18).

9. He rose up early and embraced the Lord with trust (verse 20). In the middle of a battle, it is so important that you and I, no matter how little sleep we get, set an alarm, get out of bed, (without entering the devil's playground by entering that dozing state), and actively put our trust in the hands of the Lord. Only then will your heart and your day be grounded or "established."

10. Before the battle was won, Jehoshaphat gave thanks to the Lord for His never ending, unfailing love (verse 21).

11. As the battle began, Jehoshaphat was singing and praising the Lord with a heart full of trust. We can't always sing or outwardly speak words of praise in a difficult situation, but as we review His promises, our hearts, minds, and perspectives can be defined by a reverent attitude of worship toward God in the midst of battle (verse 22).

12. As they sang praises, the Lord "sent ambushes against" the enemy and they were routed, destroying each other (verses 22 & 23).

13. Jehoshaphat and his people benefited greatly from the experience of having to face and fight in a battle where the Lord was the only hope of victory (verse 25).

14. They rejoiced greatly and marked this place of victory in their lives with a name. It is important to memorialize in your journal, your Bible, or on a list somewhere, the victories that the Lord gives you. These will give you increased confidence for battles in the future (verses 26 & 27).

15. Repeat as necessary!

Whenever we feel overwhelmed by our problems, our workload, our weaknesses, or our failures, let's remember the pattern of King Jehoshaphat and how he responded to this tremendous crisis in his life. We need to face what is in front of us with faith and humility, remembering that the outcome of the battle is not in our hands, but in the hands of God.

When we submit control of our lives to God, He loves to bless His children with the trust and courage to do our part in the battle we are fighting, so that we can learn from Him how to move from a life of fear or aggression to a life of boldly and humbly serving others and honoring Him.

Discipleship

You have probably heard before that one of the best ways to learn something is to teach it. Similarly, one of the best ways to maintain your grip on truth is to give it away to others. This is one of the reasons the Lord said in Matthew 28:19, "Go, therefore, and make disciples. . . ." When we follow this command, we grow as disciples of Christ more and more over time. One of the best ways to see the redemptive side of what you have been through is to spend an hour or a few hours a week investing in someone else.

Like Jim Lyon, the doctor who discipled me once a week over breakfast, you, too, can take what God has taught you and pass it along to someone else. Don't think that you have to know all the answers to every question to begin. Just find someone who is a little bit behind where you are in life and walk alongside them each week, caring for them, listening to them, and sharing with them what God has shared with you.

Sometimes we are tempted to believe that, because of our wounds and mistakes, we don't have anything to give others. That's a lie from the pit. We need to give back and be generous to those around us with what we have been given by others and God. I'm not talking about just getting busy or ignoring our inner battles to try to prove something. I'm talking about shifting our focus off ourselves so that we can begin experiencing the satisfaction of bringing life and joy to others.

Often we are tempted to take control or brag about ourselves to try to feel better about who we are. We think that ego and self-centeredness are going to help our insecurities, but all of this simply drives us deeper into our own problems. Jesus said in Luke 14:11, "For everyone who exalts himself will be humbled, and he who humbles himself will be exalted."

2 Timothy 2:2 says, "The things which you have heard from me in the presence of many witnesses, entrust these to faithful men who will be able to teach others also." There are four generations in this verse! This is a beautiful picture of discipleship.

If you are looking for a guide on what discipleship is all about, our book, *Eternal Impact: Investing In the Lives of Others*, might be a helpful place to start. It outlines the hows, whys, whens, wheres, and whos of discipleship. In any case, I hope you will give investing in others a try. It was the last word of instruction Jesus Christ gave to us while He was on earth, and I have found it to be incredibly rewarding.

Many years ago, as I began to invest in others, people started to come back to me and tell me what a difference those times together had made in their lives. Soon I began to see some of the value of the war I had been through. I began to see some good come out of John's horrible death.

We didn't win the war in Viet Nam, but through what I have learned as a result of being in it, I have seen people who are going to live forever because they won the war of eternity. John Atkinson is living forever in the lives of countless people who have come to know new life in Jesus Christ because of how his example, his life, and his death have impacted me.

Friend, I hope you too will begin to believe that God has a plan for your life as well. He desires to bring beauty and goodness out of even your worst experiences. I am living proof that we cannot make it alone or solve our own problems by the strength or wisdom of man. I invite you to join me in the greatest journey there is—a journey taken as a follower of Christ and a leader of anyone who will follow you toward a whole new way of life.

The Road Ahead

I am so grateful God never gave up on me. The life that I am blessed to enjoy now in my work and with my family and friends was unimaginable a few decades ago. When I have a tough day from time to time now, I am reminded there is more road to be travelled ahead and more comfort and companionship in God to be experienced.

No matter how much healing and growth God has brought into my life and heart, there is always more He wants to offer me. The storehouses of the Lord are never empty, and to the person of faith and obedience, they are never closed.

So friend, I invite you and I challenge you never to give up. When the days seem dark and our memories and broken places close in, let's call out to God with the words of King David in Psalm 62:1-2, "From the ends of the earth I call to you, I call as my heart grows faint; lead me to the rock that is higher than I. For You have been my refuge, a strong tower against the foe."

When we wonder if we have what it takes to make it, to see our lives and relationships get a fresh start, let's remember that we are not the ones who must bear the burden of our own struggles. God Himself invites us to come to Him for the love and safety and unconditional embrace we so desperately need and which only He can supply.

As you continue to learn what it means to take everything to the heart of God, make Lamentations 3:21-26 the guiding prayer of your life and the safeguard of your mind:

Yet this I call to mind

And therefore I have hope:

Because of the Lord's great love we are not consumed,

for His compassions never fail.

They are new every morning;

great is Your faithfulness.

I say to myself, 'The Lord is my portion;

therefore I will wait for Him.'

The Lord is good to those whose hope is in Him,

to the one who seeks Him;

it is good to wait quietly

for the salvation of the Lord.

Questions For Reflection

1. How many times per week do past negative or traumatic events consciously come to your mind?

2. How many times per week do past painful experiences impact you in some way emotionally?

3. Do these memories or emotions produce negative thoughts in your mind that you can identify? If so, what are some examples?

4. Have you ever noticed how one thought can be completely pushed out of your mind by another more powerful thought? Have you ever tried using this principle to expel destructive memories from your mind with Scripture?

5. What passages of Scripture mean the most to you and would be best suited to counteract the specific attacks you experience on your peace of mind?

6. Have you ever gone back to places or people associated with your past pain? If so, was this encounter a mostly positive or negative experience? Explain.

7. What circumstantial, relational, or media-related boundaries have you learned to honor in your life to help you deal with the things you have experienced and to avoid compounding them?

8. Do you ever struggle with being controlling or too aggressive? What do you think the difference is between these behaviors and the gentle boldness of a healthy initiative-taker?

9. Do you ever feel threatened, out of control, and surrounded like Jehoshaphat did?

10. What stood out to you most about Jehoshaphat's response to his situation?

11. Who are two people to whom you could begin to open up in a deeper way than you have before, about the things with which you are struggling and working on learning right now?

12. Who is someone you know who has also experienced significant life pain whom you would be able to begin encouraging?

CHAPTER FIVE

Daughter of a Soldier
A Relationship Restored

by Anna Downer

I grew up as the fourth of six children and the older twin sister of an outgoing, gregarious brother. My family was expressive and intense—a stark contrast to my quiet and timid demeanor. I always connected well with my measured, soft-spoken mother, but my loud and animated father scared me from the time I was a baby.

When I was about five Dad asked me what kind of man I wanted to marry someday, and I replied, "A very quiet one." Perhaps this was part of the reason my relationship with him was distant in my early years. In addition to the personality differences between us, I remember hearing from a young age intense stories from his war days in Viet Nam. The war had long since been over for America, but there was a very real battle happening in our home. Though we weren't the enemy, sometimes Dad misdirected the pain, fear, and anger he had from the war and his past toward those who were closest to him.

I remember sometimes feeling like there were two dads in our house—one who came home from work with a loud and happy "Hellooo, kids!" and made his way through the kitchen hugging us, kissing Mom and making jokes. Then there was the other dad who communicated with the way he opened the door that he was stressed and on the edge of losing his temper, and that we kids would need to tip-toe around the house for the rest of the night to keep him from getting upset.

I can't remember a time I doubted that the fun, relaxed Dad loved me—The Dad who played on the floor with us, took us camping, and taught us baseball and softball. But as a child I felt caught between this knowledge of his love and my fear of his sometimes explosive anger.

Something small or seemingly nothing at all would set him off. He could go from being relaxed and happy, to raging with anger, faster than I could figure out what had upset him. In hindsight I see that it wasn't so much the exterior circumstances that made him angry but rather something inside of him. As a child that never occurred to me—I was just afraid of him, and eventually, angry that he made me afraid.

I remember one time I came downstairs at night to get a drink of water and heard him yelling at Mom in their room. I heard the familiar sound of him flinging the bedroom door open and so I retreated into the closet as he thundered through the kitchen. I trembled with fear as he banged around the kitchen and eventually left the house. I waited until I knew he was long gone before making my way back to my room.

Though it seems obvious now, as a little girl I didn't understand that I wasn't the source of his anger. I withdrew from our relationship out of uncertainty and fear. It took me years to admit I was angry with Dad, an emotion I avoided out of a desire not to be like him. Distancing myself from Dad no doubt communicated that I didn't want him to be involved in my life. This caused Dad a lot of pain, but the harder he tried to make me open up to him and be affectionate, the more I resisted his pressure and pulled away.

Perhaps you have had similar struggles in your relationship with a daughter or son. Maybe, like my dad, you have wondered if your child even wanted you involved in his or her life, and if it would ever be possible to heal the relational rift between you.

The truth is, as broken as our relationship was, what I wanted more than anything was to be close to my father. I desperately wanted him to be a safe place for me. I wanted to forgive, but I was afraid that he would never change. Looking back on our relationship in my grade school years, the situation seemed hopeless to me. But as a result of key principles that Dad resolutely followed, my willingness to forgive, and the grace of God to us both, the Lord has brought incredible healing and restoration to our relationship. No matter what your relationship is like with your daughter or son, God desires, and is capable of, bringing redemption to it.

The Road to Restoration

One of the first steps Dad took to begin rebuilding our relationship was to find ways to communicate that he was interested in the things that were important to me. When I was five, I remember he came up to my room and sat down on the floor where we played with the dolls in my dollhouse together. I have this vivid memory of watching him try to sit down in several different positions, testing which was least painful for his bad knees. I may have been young, but I knew that my Dad hated sitting on the floor and playing with dolls—but that he loved me.

Parents, don't underestimate how much your daughter or son wants to be close to you! They may not show it or able to articulate it, but it is one of the strongest desires of their heart. I had a friend I will call Amy, who had practically no relationship with her father and didn't seem to be bothered by it. Her dad lived with the family, but he never tried to get involved in her life or ask how her day was. In high school she was constantly dating, yet she seemed unemotional and flippant about her many boyfriends and her dad's emotional absence.

One day I struck up a conversation with Amy about her father and she admitted how painful it was that he never told her he loved her. She said, "Anna, the only way I know my father loves me is because of the new car he bought me. I'm finally realizing that I'm dating all these guys just to find the attention and affirmation I have never had from my dad." Your daughters don't just want what you can buy them; they want the acceptance and relationship that a parent is uniquely designed to give.

Friendship

Another way Dad communicated love to me was by his perseverance in pursuing a natural, personal friendship with me through conversation. When I was eight, I remember Dad taking me out to Subway for lunch. Apparently he told Mom he wasn't going to come back until we had a real conversation.

As we sat eating, Dad began to ask me questions about my life and I quietly responded with one-word answers. Dad gently continued asking question after question until I realized, "Wow, Dad is actually interested." When I finally believed this, I began opening up to him about the books I was reading, the things I was learning in school, what made me happy and what made me sad. It was his kind and gentle persistence that earned my trust.

This was just the beginning of a closer relationship—though it wasn't all smooth sailing. There were still many painful events to occur, but that day stands out in my mind as a significant step forward. It was a day I believed and experienced Dad's care for me and his interest in what was important to me, a vital component to a close relationship with anyone.

Dads, don't miss out on learning how to dialogue with your daughters. It is vital for you to listen to our opinions and to affirm the value of our perspective, especially as we get older. I know it was tempting for my dad to feel like he always had to be instructing me so that I didn't make a mistake. But sometimes we daughters just need a listening ear. When you take the time and energy to listen to our ideas and affirm our uniqueness and contribution to a decision, process, or discussion, you show us trust and respect, earning ours in return.

Love Without Fear

Another key to building a strong relationship with your child is to have an attitude of faith, rather than fear. This is something my father really struggled with in our relationship, especially during my early years. It was so ingrained in him from his war days to motivate out of fear and he struggled with so much fear himself, that his actions toward me often came across as heavy-handed and controlling.

He saw a lot of himself in me as a child—my propensity to fear, to handle conflict badly, and to react in emotion. These were all struggles of his own that had caused him a lot of pain. Wanting to keep me from making the same mistakes, Dad tried to teach me how to master my emotions and keep them from ruling my life.

While I now understand that his motive was to help me, his method of doing so often came from his own fear, making his efforts very hurtful. I was a sensitive, fearful girl. Yelling at me for crying was not exactly a good way to keep me from crying. I grew up feeling like something was wrong with me, and that I needed to fundamentally change who I was in order to be "OK" in Dad's eyes. His desire to change me was for my best, but to a little girl who didn't understand the complexity of her father's heart for her, his correction came across as rejection of some of the things that made me uniquely me.

The summer after my first year of college was a struggle for me. I was working through some of these issues for the first time and was at a loss as to how to find healing from the performance-focus and perfectionism that I found constantly eating away at my joy.

With only good intentions, Dad took me out and lectured me for several hours on how he thought I should fix the issues I was facing. From his perspective, he was trying to help me overcome my problems and find solutions—what father wouldn't want to help his daughter? But from my perspective, his advice and warnings came across as criticisms and expectations. His didactic, authoritative lectures were really a response to his own fear over how much I was struggling and the guilt he felt for the role he may have had in causing some of my pain.

What I needed more than anything that night was for Dad to see me in all my failure and mess and brokenness and simply claim me as his own. I didn't need him to try to change or fix me. I needed his unconditional love and acceptance.

Although Dad hasn't always been perfect at communicating his acceptance of me, I have many memories of times when he poignantly demonstrated unconditional love. When I was about 13, Dad took me on a date and was talking to me about boys and relationships and standards. I remember how kindly and gently he talked about the wisdom of staying pure and the pain he had experienced from the mistakes he had made as a teenager.

At the end of our lunch he turned to me and said, "Anna, no matter what you do, no matter if you make a huge mistake and get pregnant before marriage or run away from Jesus, you will always be my daughter. You will always be welcome in my house, and I will always love you."

Dad demonstrated in many other ways his love for me that was not based on my performance, such as his faithfulness to keep coming to my softball games even when I was a terrible player. I almost hated seeing him there because I was so ashamed of how bad I was. I thought he would much prefer to be watching my All-Star twin at his games. In those moments I was battling the idea that my value in my dad's eyes, and in life in general, was something I had to earn through my performance. By coming to every one of my games and cheering for me loudly from the stands no matter how badly I played, Dad reinforced for me the truth that my security and value in our relationship was unshakeable.

Dad has grown immensely in learning how to respond to our relationship out of faith, rather than fear. As his confidence and peace grew in his relationship with God, that attitude of trust and rest spilled over into our relationship. When I went to Spain for three months with a good friend during college, Dad gave me some advice and warnings before I went, but then trusted me to go. He also turned into the Encourager Extraordinaire—I have countless voicemails saved on my phone with Dad's cheery voice calling to say he loved me and was praying for me.

My Role

In addition to Dad working to love me well and understand me better, I also worked at understanding him. It took me years to realize that as I was growing up, Dad's anger wasn't directly proportionate to whatever I had just said or done. Sometimes when he would explode, it wasn't at all about the comment I had just made. Before I realized this, however, I would react in ways that were hurtful to him.

It seemed insignificant to me that I didn't feel like going downstairs to welcome him home from work or that I sometimes didn't feel like talking to him when he came in the room. But often these behaviors triggered his anger because they reminded him of the trauma in his relationship with his parents, the lack of affirmation he experienced in his childhood, and even the close friends he lost in combat. So much of Dad's anger was a direct result of his deep pain—and only the healing of God could salve that wound.

As a daughter, I needed to learn to be more considerate of him. I began to grow in this way, but I knew I couldn't fix his pain. I had to allow myself the freedom of accepting that I was not responsible for everything that hurt my father. In turn, Dad began to learn how to manage his instinctive emotional responses when something would upset him.

Dad learned to ask questions about what I meant to say in order to draw out the thoughts and motives of his sometimes subdued daughter. He learned to find out what I was thinking before reacting on impulse. Over time, our understanding of each other grew, and we began to see past our misunderstandings and differences to the genuine love we each had for the other.

The Work of Reconciliation

Perhaps the most important thing Dad did to heal our relationship was to learn to apologize. By apologize I don't mean just saying "Sorry" and walking out of the room. Dad nearly made apologies into an art form. When Dad saw how his actions had caused me pain, he would take time to sit down with me and walk through what he had done wrong and apologize for it specifically.

For example, Dad would say, "Anna, when I came into the room just now I was feeling a lot of pressure and anxiety for reasons that had nothing to do with you at all. That is why I snapped at you. It was not your fault. I am so sorry I reacted that way. Please forgive me." He would ask for my forgiveness and I would forgive him, and then a few days later he would follow up and ask how I was doing and apologize again.

This part was especially important as it can sometimes take me days to actually process and respond to a life experience on an emotional level. When Dad would make the same mistake again, his genuine remorse and efforts to spend time with me to rebuild my trust always turned my heart back to him again.

In my middle school years, Dad went a step further. Even without any recent conflict, he would ask me if there was anything he had done lately to hurt me. If there was, he would apologize for it. At first I was shocked—did he actually mean it? It took me years before I trusted him enough to be completely honest with him and take the risk that he would not get angry at me for my honesty. He rebuilt my trust one apology, one date, one encouraging word at a time. So I took him up on his offer and began to be more open with him than I had ever been before.

At the end of my junior year of high school, I remember waking up to Dad screaming at Josh, my twin, and me to come downstairs. He lined us up in the kitchen and yelled at us for what felt like 30 minutes about how disastrous the house looked and what a bad job we were doing of keeping things organized. He was our drill instructor, and we took it like recruits. But I was crushed.

The next day Dad apologized, as I knew he would. I forgave him, as I knew I should, but I also looked him in the eye and calmly said, "Dad, you can be my DI, or you can be my father. But if you want to be my father, you can't ever treat me like that again." That was incredibly hard for me to do because first, I was afraid of what he would say, and second, I knew it would hurt him to hear that. But it was true, and he needed to hear it.

Dad took it very calmly and apologized, and came back around every few days for weeks to apologize again and comfort the pain and fear I still had from the incident. His humble and open response made me realize how much his heart was in the right place, and how much he regretted the times when his emotions and tongue got out of control.

The Gift of Grace

Dad's persistence to apologize and work to heal the wounds he had caused were a priceless model to me for how to give and receive grace. I have come to believe there is nothing more essential to relationships than understanding they are grace-based. None of us can live in healthy relationships with others without giving them grace for their sins and receiving grace for ours.

Dad had the wisdom and humility not to hide his mistakes from me, but to be honest and humble enough to confess them and, in this way, demonstrate his need for God's forgiveness and for mine. This softened my heart toward him so that even in the midst of being hurt by his failures, I was willing to extend grace and forgiveness. Because Dad had so faithfully modeled for me how to receive grace for himself, I was open to allowing him into my life when I made mistakes. Dad is one of the most grace-filled people I know, and I am grateful to have been on the receiving end of his grace-giving many times. Dad has been a picture of my Heavenly Father in that he has never been stingy with grace. I can't remember a time he didn't forgive me for something I had done wrong.

Throughout his years as a Christian, Dad's understanding of grace has broadened and deepened, and in turn he has modeled it to us as his children. One instance that demonstrates this is a time when all six of us kids behaved terribly one day and Mom was just fed up. She called Dad and said, "Honey, when you come home from work you need to spank them all!" So Dad came home and lined us up in my brother Matt's room.

We were all standing at attention, braced for imminent discipline when he started his speech. He said, "You know, kids, I really haven't spent enough time with you lately. Instead of spanking you, even though you deserve it, let's go out for ice cream and hang out." I remember thinking, "That was the best spanking ever!" But beyond the relief of escaping discipline, I'll never forget the time we deserved to be disciplined, but received grace instead.

Dad was teaching us the truth that when you're in relationship with God and God's people, sometimes you *don't* get what you deserve when you do something wrong. Feeling a sense of amazement, gratefulness, and humility in the face of something so undeserved is the key to understanding the beauty of the Gospel. The gift of the Gospel is not something we deserve or have earned. God forgives us immeasurably more than we can comprehend.

Just like Dad did in this instance, God lavishes His grace on us without measure. The power of grace has enabled Dad and I to forgive ourselves and each other for the many mistakes we have made and the pain we have caused. Relationships aren't about perfection. If they were, none of us would have a chance! I think that Dad chose to impress that principle upon us because he relied on grace so much in his life.

Beauty From Ashes

As Dad continued to spend one-on-one time with me, apologize when he got upset, and model grace, he built a strong trust between us. I respect my father more than any man I know. Throughout my years in high school and college, I began to seek him out for advice and counsel, and our friendship really deepened. He became my first call when I needed encouragement or relationship advice. He was also quick to remind me that God's unconditional, unshakable love is the answer and the hope for the intense perfectionism I have battled over the years.

I have come to trust him with the most personal things happening in my life—and it's not because he's perfect! My father is a man who has been humbled and reshaped by the love of God. I have invited him more and more into my life over these years because I know I can truly trust him and that he has my best interests at heart. I know this is true even when he has made mistakes. When I look at my past, Dad has demonstrated his faithful love for me in every date he's taken me on, every time he has called to encourage me, and each conversation in which he has prayed for my upcoming tests. I was also grateful that when praying for my tests, he would say in the next breath that he would love me no matter the result.

We daughters aren't looking for perfection—Dads, we know you're not perfect and we aren't either! But because of my father's humility and love in forgiving me and working through whatever issues we have had to face together, he has built a storehouse of trust in my heart for him.

To the same degree that he has been able to receive grace from God for his own sin and pain, he has been able to give it to others, including me. His many choices to pursue healing through his relationship with Christ have modeled that process to me. I have seen what it takes to heal from childhood pain, and as I have followed my dad's example in my own walk with the Lord, I have also experienced the comfort and healing that God offers to all of us.

As a daughter, I have also learned how to communicate love and acceptance to my father. I have realized that when I have not given him the encouragement he desperately needed to hear from me, it was only out of my selfish stubbornness. As I have gotten older, God has shown me my sin of being stingy with grace toward him in refusing to thank him for things he has done for me or how hard he has worked for our family. As children, it is so important to do this for our dads. It is such a gift to them to express how much we value their hard work and their role in our lives.

It is never easy to forgive. There have been many times when I haven't felt like forgiving Dad. I may have said that I forgave him, but inside I knew I was still harboring anger and resentment toward him. Over time, the more God increased my awareness of my own need for forgiveness from Him and others, the more He softened my heart to extend forgiveness toward my father.

I also sensed God asking me to go a step further—not only to forgive, but to learn to really trust him again, without reservation. It would have been easy to forgive Dad and yet keep him at arms length for the rest of my life. Perhaps some would have said I had "the right" to do so. But I have no doubt that if I had chosen that path, then our resulting lack of relationship would have been one of the biggest and most painful regrets of my life.

Dad and I now have a relationship built on mutual forgiveness, love, and trust. Coming to this place of restoration in our relationship took years of cultivation and healing that can only come from God. Now that my friendship with my dad has become such a treasure in my life, I wouldn't trade it for anything in the world.

Questions For Reflection

1. As a daughter, what made relating to your dad difficult when you were young? What was your response?

2. As a father, what attitudes and behavior patterns in your daughter's life have created conflict between you?

3. What are the best memories you have of being together?

4. What would you say it looks like to experience love without fear?

5. What is one thing you wish was more a part of your father-daughter relationship?

6. If you could change or remove anything in your father-daughter relationship, what would it be?

7. As a father, what are some interests or hobbies in your daughter's life to which you could begin directing some of your time and attention?

8. As a daughter, how could you begin expressing a new level of respect and gratitude toward your father?

9. What would it look like if your father-daughter relationship began to be less defined by blame and resentment and more covered in grace?

10. What is one practical step you could take right now to begin expressing a new level of forgiveness, grace, and hope in your father-daughter relationship?

CHAPTER SIX

Collateral Damage
Rebuilding A Father-Son Relationship

by Paul Downer

One afternoon in college, I saw a buddy of mine walking down the hallway in our dorm when I noticed he was limping and looked a little disoriented. I knew he played rugby, but he really seemed banged up. "Brett, what happened to you? You don't look so good," I said.

"Oh hey, Paul. I'm good, man," he said. But I could tell that beneath his carefree grin, he was in a lot of pain.

"No seriously, what'd you do to yourself?" I asked him. Brett turned around and told me the story.

He had been riding his motorcycle when suddenly his helmet flew off. (Brett liked to drive fast. Really fast.) After parking his bike on the side of the road, he walked back to where his helmet was sitting in the middle of the street just over a hill. As Brett bent over to pick it up, with no warning, a driver crested the hill and smashed into Brett's butt at full speed! The impact flipped Brett onto the hood where he sank into the windshield of the car. For a split second the driver was too stunned to react, so she didn't stop! Then she realized, "I've hit a human being!" at which point she did what any of us would have done—she stomped on her brakes!

I doubt this is how Brett had always imagined his first experience with human flight. As the car screeched to a halt, Brett launched out of the windshield leaving a spray of glass in his wake as he sailed through the air and tumbled to the pavement in a heap. Despite the driver's earnest protests, Brett insisted he was fine to go home, retrieved his helmet for a second time, and made his way back to campus.

"Brett, you were just in a head-on collision between a car and your body!" I said. "Why aren't you in the hospital getting checked out for internal injuries, bleeding, and who knows what?"

"Dude, it's no big deal, I'm good," he said, and limped out the door.

Like I did, you might be asking yourself how someone can walk away from getting hit by a car like it's nothing. But the truth is, a lot of us go through life doing the very same thing.

Walking Wounded

As the insurance commercial says, *Life comes at you fast!* And much of what comes at you is not all that great. Soon after we are born, we begin trying to understand the world around us. It's a world of sights and shapes and sounds that invites us to explore and experience.

As toddlers and then as young children, we begin figuring out how some of the pieces fit together. On a deeper level, whether spoken or only felt, we start to ask one of the most fundamental human questions. *What can I expect out of life?*

We are optimistic at first. But then the day comes when, for the very first time, we are burned. We bounce back, hoping it was a one-time experience. But then our world, which had seemed so dependably warm and inviting, bites us again—and again. And more than recoiling once or twice, we *learn* to recoil. We learn to doubt. No one is born afraid, but threatened and hurt enough, the natural instinct of anyone is to embrace fear as the only logical response. Eventually the truth sinks in, that for all its virtues and beauty, this world isn't always a very safe place.

Though my parents had begun a relationship with Christ six years before I was born, they were still early in their spiritual journeys by the time I came around. As the eldest boy in my family, I got along fine with my mom but clashed regularly with my dad. In addition to our personality differences, I felt a lot of stress and pressure when I was around him and I didn't know how to deal with it.

It never occurred to me how much better my dad was doing as a father than the model he'd been given growing up. I didn't give him much credit for what he was learning each passing year about taking his struggles to God. I only saw the remaining tension and anger that spilled over on me when things went wrong.

By the time I was twelve, I was hurt and bitter. I was tired of his anger, his criticism, and the anxiety of never knowing when the tensions in his own life were going to boil into frustration, arguments, and conflicts at home. He had been trained in the Marine Corps; I felt like I was being raised in the Marine Corps. Sometimes hearing that Dad was on his way home from work didn't feel like good news to me. There was a distance between us that was growing wider and wider.

As a part of my work with Discipleship Network of America, I spend a great deal of time with high school students. These students have countless stories that are just heartbreaking—stories far worse than mine. In our culture, a childhood that is free of some kind of significant pain is by far the exception rather than the rule. As children, once we have begun to experience hurt and brokenness and the fear that accompanies them, few of us are capable of unpacking or understanding our experiences. We instinctively move on and try our best to live a "normal" life.

This "normal" life, however, is not what it might have been. Without thinking about it, many kids respond to their childhood hurts and pressures by becoming nonconformists and mavericks. Their actions scream that they don't care.

But it's a farce, a hollow bluff in a high stakes game of chicken between the still-tender heart of a child and a threatening world they cannot appease, control, or understand. Whether because of anger, bullying, racism, abuse, or abandonment, they have learned early that hoping for consistent acceptance or affirmation is naive. So they live with ever-lower expectations and hearts dressed in armor, determined that any sense of identity or value will be self-defined.

Others, rather than bucking the system, become "yes men"— pliable conformists who try to beat the system from the inside by living life by the rules. Some take this to greater extremes than others. But the general approach of conformists is to be compliant, apologetic, and non-confrontational, constantly striving to discern and fulfill the expectations they sense surrounding them. Around their peers, conformity is an attempt to blend in and be accepted, to follow the established attitudes and behaviors that are typical for that circle of friends.

Conformists may also strive to fit the preferences and fulfill the requirements of their authorities. Their resulting exemplary performance is not a sign of maturity, high character, or self-confidence, however. It is a down payment on the elusive prize of affirmation that authority figures only seem to offer with the price tag of good behavior.

Does this mean that whenever you see kids conforming to, or resisting, the expectations around them, that these behaviors are always merely the product of their woundedness? No, not necessarily. But this is the case if their choices are merely attempts to prop up their sense of self.

Like droves of kids today, I was a combination of both extremes. There were times when I lived like a maverick, striking out in anger and rebellion. Other times I was a "yes man," trying as hard as I could to conform my words, attitudes, and actions to the expectations I felt around me, especially those coming from my dad. Over time, like many kids, I became more and more confused in my dual posture toward life, alternating erratically between blind conformity and bitter resistance, depending on the context.

However, regardless of which persona I lived out on a given day, I walked through life like Brett after he was hit by that car—dismissive toward my past experiences and the inner brokenness they may have produced in my life. Unbeknownst to me, at a young age, I had already joined the latest generation of the walking wounded. It would be years before I began to understand this fact and learn how God was already planning my rescue.

Escapism Is No Escape

During my early childhood years, I spent little time reflecting on my relationship problems with my dad. Regardless of your age, perhaps you can relate to this. For a host of reasons, many of us do our best to ignore the hard things we have experienced. We bury our painful memories, avoid our dysfunctional relationships and do our best to simply live life. Sooner or later, however, most of us discover a fundamental truth: escapism is no escape. The things we run from drive us. Eventually, that which drives us, defines us.

Even when I was just ten and eleven years old, I could tell somehow that my life was not headed in the right direction. Something was wrong, and not just with Dad. Something was wrong with me. I had developed many of the characteristics I most resented in my dad—and more.

Like Dad, I had become increasingly impatient, irritable, and moody. But unlike Dad, I was also becoming a bully, dishonest, and a slacker, the kind of guy who always looks for short cuts and the easy way out. If there was a conflict around me, especially in my family, I was in the middle of it, yelling and swinging.

Then I hit puberty and things got even more complicated. The idea of controlling my thoughts and eyes and living in sexual purity seemed impossible to me.

As I began to resemble more and more the typical kind of rebellious kid that our culture has so often come to expect, my dad was getting more and more nervous about where I was headed. Though I still felt fully justified in pointing out his flaws, I was meanwhile duplicating and expanding on them in my own life. So far, my attempts to cope with and get past my problems on my own were going nowhere.

Imagine the Possibilities

In Romans 4:17, the Apostle Paul describes God as the one who "brings life to the dead and calls into being that which does not exist." This is an astonishing statement. Paul knew what he was talking about, too. When the risen Christ stopped him dead in his tracks on the road to Damascus, his spiritual life didn't have a pulse. It was all self-centered bravado and cold, religious zeal. Through this face-to-face encounter with Jesus and the terror of three days and nights of blindness, God showed him the morbid state of his spiritual condition and brought a new birth of faith to his soul. His life was never the same.

Pause for a minute and ask yourself: Where in my life do I feel helpless, at a dead end, or in the dark? Do I have old, unresolved wounds that have compromised my peace of mind and joy in life? Has anxiety or resentment drained the life out of my relationships? For too many of us, the hurts and wounds that come to our minds concern our relationships with our fathers and our sons.

There is something about the father-son relationship that is incredibly important in the life of a man. Romans 4:17 means that God can and does enter into the dead and dying places in our lives and relationships and call them into vibrant being. It is a miracle, a beautiful collision between the powerful love of God and our brokenness.

This is not to say that God will always restore everything that is broken in our lives. Some sons have never met their fathers. For others, their fathers are no longer alive. In these cases, as with my dad whose father died before I was born, the path to healing is one to which God can guide a man even in the absence of his earthly father.

But for the rest of us whose fathers are still alive, this verse dares us to expand what we think could even be possible; to hope that the Creator and Sustainer of the entire cosmos could still raise to life a weak, ailing, or seemingly dead father-son relationship. We live in a time when most people are running low on faith and have no shortage of cynicism.o Our most common mistake is that we seek the powerful intervention of God in our lives too little, not too much.

Even without our invitation, however, our Heavenly Father is always faithfully at work all around us. God never forsakes His renewing, remaking activity in the world or in the lives of His children. As Philippians 2:13 says, "It is God who works in you to will and to act according to His good purpose."

Yet, we have been created and shaped by God specifically for a relationship with Him. He desires our responsiveness and our active participation with Him as He works to bring healing and newness into our lives. He longs for us to invite Him to do, in and around us, what we could never do on our own.

Fatal Errors

As we try to understand our role in God's renewing work, we can get stuck in one of two places. On the one hand, many of us are so hurt, frustrated, and discouraged by what we have experienced that we are unable to consider the possibility that our situation could ever improve.

As Proverbs 13:12 says, "Hope deferred makes the heart sick." Tired of being disappointed, we begin to view hope as a liability, a piece of cargo too heavy for such choppy seas. So we toss it overboard and resign ourselves to the grimness of life as we try just to ride out the storm. Even at twelve years of age this is nearly where I was. It was very hard for me to picture my life or my relationship with my dad improving.

Instead of succumbing to despair, others of us bolster our courage by telling ourselves that we can overcome our hurts and relational conflicts on our own. We become diligent collectors of elaborate strategies which we believe will enable us to turn back the tide of brokenness and division around us.

As helpful as such resources can be, the fundamental flaw of this approach is that it places our confidence in ourselves independent of God. In America, the personal quality of independence is viewed as being a strength, even a virtue—and in some contexts this may be warranted. But a life of self-reliance in spiritual terms is nothing less than a cancer and is portrayed in Scripture in the harshest possible light. Jeremiah 17:5-6 paints the picture this way:

> Cursed is the one who trusts in man, who depends on flesh for his strength and whose heart turns away from the Lord. He will be like a bush in the wastelands; he will not see prosperity when it comes. He will dwell in the parched places of the desert, in a salt land where no one lives.

God has no interest in watching us reshape our problems into monuments of human self-sufficiency. This would be to lift up as a "solution" the very lie that brought sin and hurt into the world in the first place. Thankfully, this is not the approach my dad chose.

The son of a man who always claimed to have *pulled himself up by his own boot straps*, my dad made calling out to God for help and strength and wisdom and direction the hallmark of his life. He knew he didn't have what it would take to turn things around in our relationship. So he began to ask God that he would be characterized by the heart, attitude, and life described in the next section of Jeremiah 17, which has this to say about a life of reliance upon God.

> But blessed is the man who trusts in the Lord, whose confidence is in him. He will be like a tree planted by the water that sends out its roots by the stream. It does not fear when heat comes; its leaves are always green. It has no worries in a year of drought and never fails to bear fruit.

This passage doesn't mean that everyone who lives a life of trust in God will never experience hardship (see 1 Peter 4:12-14). But without question, there is a quality of fullness and vibrancy in life that only accompanies those who live in step with God, while relying on His promises and being expectant toward His provision.

Dad had chosen this life of Godward trust before I was even born. Now he was beginning to ask God to teach him in a fresh way how to father me as God had been fathering him. As Dad began to invite God to rebuild our relationship, He did incredible things in both of us. But Dad had a crucial part in this as well.

I would like to share with you seven things Dad did that impacted our relationship the most.

Dad Didn't Give Up On Me.

Not yet having any children of my own, I have no idea what it is like to be the father of an angry, resentful, ungrateful son. But my dad sure does. During recent years, I have heard him express honestly how frustrating this was for him. He has shared how discouraging it was that I always took Mom's side in arguments and only seemed to notice the things he did wrong, throwing the best he could do back in his face. But by the grace of God and out of his love for me, Dad didn't write me off. He determined that, no matter the cost, our relationship was worth fighting for and he would do so through the strength and love of God.

Of all the decisions that have been made by anyone in my life, this is the one that has impacted me the most. Fathers, you have been given a powerful authority in our lives by God, as your sons. In some mysterious way, God has given you an unrivaled ability to contribute to and strengthen our qualities of confidence, boldness, and courage. No father accomplishes this perfectly, of course. I if God blesses me with sons one day, I know that I will be no exception. But know that whether through your words or your actions, every time you share your heart, wisdom, and affirmation with your sons, it falls like rain on thirsty ground.

Even before we learn that we have a Father in heaven, we sons encounter His representative in you. By giving you the role and title of "father" in our lives, God has assigned you the unique task of picturing to us what He is like and how He views us. We look to you for direction, answers, and approval, years before we ever learn to look to Him for these things.

I wish we made this task easier on you. If the time has not yet arrived, I hope there comes a day when your son begins to appreciate the gifts you have given him as a father. But this much I do know: regardless of your story and whether you have many regrets or few, you are worthy of respect. You are worthy of honor for everything you have sacrificed to love us, to invest in us, and to equip us for life. No matter how small or how great your role has been in our lives, thank you for what you have given. Without it, our lives would be so much less.

You were the one through whom God brought us into the world. When you were there for us, you could have been elsewhere. When you showed us by your time and attention that we are loved and valuable, you could have passed us by. Every kindness you have shown us has been mortar to our foundations. We hold our lives together better and stand taller because of you. For that alone, you are deserving of honor.

No matter what your situation is, if your son is alive today then your story is not over. Your legacy is not yet set in stone.

There is still time for God to rewrite the coming paragraphs and chapters of your relationship. A story is not defined by its beginning, but by its ending. On behalf of your sons, please don't give up on us.

We might be pushing you away right now, pretending we have it all together and that we don't want to have anything to do with you. Don't be fooled by this facade. It is a hollow defense, a superficial layer of self-protectiveness that masks our need for you in our lives, our unspoken desire that you might step further into a relationship with us. Should God be willing to bless your obedience to Him in your relationship with your son, then the legacy of this restoration will endure for many generations to come. The rewritten narrative of your relationship with your son will become the celebrated prequel to every story after it.

This process will not be easy. It never is. Judging from what I put my own father through, I expect it will be risky and hard. The heart of a son is a difficult and precious thing to win. But for us sons, there is no earthly gift more sacred than the love and blessing of our dad. For the part my dad has played in my story, he will forever be my greatest hero.

While some of us are not dads yet, we are of course all sons. This story is not just for fathers, but also for us as sons. No matter how old your father is, you have a unique role to play in your relationship with him as well. At any point along the road toward reconciliation between my dad and me, I could have hijacked the whole thing. But I didn't. I followed his example and learned to let God lead me just as He had led him.

Dad Was Committed to Saying: I Was Wrong, I'm Sorry, Will You Forgive Me?

As Dad prayed that God would show him how to improve things between us, he realized the best place to start was to get real with me in the most practical way possible. One of the top complaints that kids have about their parents is that they aren't authentic and don't admit their flaws and mistakes nearly as often as they bring up those of their children. Unfortunately, whether this hypocrisy is real or perceived or a mixture of both, it is often used by kids as an excuse to be disrespectful toward their parents and shut them out.

Rather than waiting for me to respect him as I should have, Dad decided that, as hard as it was going to be, he needed to make the first move by admitting to me and to our family when he messed up. Early on, I had no idea how hard this was for him to do. As an attorney, he must have been tempted to simply defend himself. But he hung in there and prayed for God's help to stay humble, remembering James 4:10, which says, "Humble yourself in the sight of the Lord, and He will lift you up."

At first it didn't really mean anything to me when he would own up to his mistakes. It just felt like empty words to me. But as he continued to live with authenticity in front of us, I started to realize he really meant what he was saying and that he wasn't excusing his anger. Slowly, my attitude toward him began to soften.

You may not think there is anything special about saying the precise words, "I was wrong. I'm sorry. Will you forgive me?" But, however you decide to word your apology and request for forgiveness, make sure it is not accompanied by excuses or accusations.

James 5:16 tells us to confess our sins to each other and pray for each other, so that we may be healed. My dad decided he was going to apply this as a lifestyle. When he would say to me, "I was wrong," without excuses or defensiveness, he was openly admitting his mistakes rather than ignoring or justifying them. He was being real and honest with me without pointing his finger at what I had done wrong.

When a parent does not verbally admit his or her mistakes, a child will often take this as hypocrisy and even dishonesty. Is this fair? No, it isn't. Not mentioning one's flaws isn't the same as lying about them. But over time, silence regarding one's weaknesses and offenses can become a mask, a relational barrier of unaddressed and unresolved conflict between you and those around you.

My dad took off his mask by breaking that silence, which required gutsy humility in his view of himself, practical obedience toward God, and sacrificial love for me. For a child, this kind of self-disclosing honesty from a parent is powerful. It disarms a child's accusations of hypocrisy and paves the way for a greater level of respect.

In addition to admitting his faults, Dad was also faithful to say to me with genuine sincerity, "I'm sorry." This communicated to me that he cared about what his anger felt like on my end and that he was genuinely putting himself in my shoes rather than flippantly saying whatever he had to say to move on. This began to break through my resentment toward him and take the edge off my bitterness.

Especially for a child, the worst part about being on the receiving end of anger is that it introduces an element of relational instability or danger. This, in turn, can undermine a child's basic sense of value, safety, and his or her capacity to trust.

Because of the trauma of my dad's childhood and his combat experiences in Viet Nam, he understood all too well the consequences of relational wounds. Due to this understanding, he was able to turn his attention from the hurts at the root of his own struggles and direct his focus to me out of genuine empathy. This made it possible for our relationship to continue to grow.

Dad also had the vulnerability to say to me: "Will you forgive me?" He asked this question because he knew that every time there was a clash between his anger and my stubborn view of my personal rights, a little more distance and tension was added between us. He recognized that if he didn't clear the offense between us by asking my forgiveness then, over time, resentment and bitterness would only continue to pile up between us.

Asking me to forgive him was also a way of drawing me into an active role in resolving our conflict. When someone is hurt or offended, they often respond by sitting back and becoming passive spectators. With the assertiveness of Dad's request for my forgiveness, he increased my level of personal investment in the process of working through our differences.

I will never forget the time I was talking to a buddy of mine in college when it suddenly dawned on him for the first time that he had grown up in a family that never fully resolved conflict— ever! Offenses and insults were just brushed aside, never cleared, confessed, or forgiven. Since graduating from high school, each day spent with his family on summer breaks or reunions had been overshadowed by the cumulative history of their unresolved arguments and disputes. It was like the relational landscape of his family had the uneasy feel of a graveyard haunted by conflicts never put to rest. This is the way my dad grew up, too, and it was a part of his story that he didn't want to repeat.

As I work with parents and teens at weekend conferences, I have noticed that many parents are reluctant to admit their mistakes to their children and ask their forgiveness for one primary reason. They worry that their vulnerability will backfire and that their children will throw their admissions back in their faces with the same disrespect that has been much of the cause of their conflicts in the first place.

Without question, in the short term, this can happen. But as your children, we already know your flaws and you already know ours. That's part of life in a family. I have seen over and over again that when parents begin a practice of admitting their mistakes, expressing empathy, and sincerely asking forgiveness, their children's respect for them doesn't decrease—it increases! Honesty and humility are powerfully disarming forces. As Dad became more vulnerable and open with me, I began to want to get real with him about my weaknesses and sin too.

Soon I was following his example. I turned my attention from the mental list I had been keeping of my dad's flaws and began to be proactive about admitting my mistakes and asking him and others for forgiveness. This was incredibly good news in my house, since of all the kids in my family, I was by far the biggest troublemaker.

Not only did Dad's example increase my respect for him and my own willingness to admit my flaws, but I also became more open to receiving his advice and input in my life. His model of humility opened my ears toward him, clearing the way for one of the most valuable treasures in the world to enter into my life: the wisdom, experience, and counsel of my dad.

Sons, if we think we don't need the input of our dads in our lives, we are dead wrong. I know that sometimes it can be tempting to write them off. It can feel like it would be easier to push them out of our lives rather than to face and work through the hurt and the messed up patterns that have taken root over the years. But that's just a cop-out, a pointless attempt to run away.

Granted, maybe your dad doesn't have a relationship with God. Or even if he does, maybe you don't think he has anything of value to teach or offer you. But that's just how things look through the eyes of resentment. Whenever we turn our backs on our fathers, claiming we have just cause because of the ways they have mistreated us, we are choosing a life of bitterness. And bitterness is a poison to the soul and venom to relationships.

Hebrews 12:15 says, "See to it that no one misses the grace of God and that no bitter root grows up to cause trouble and defile many." The cruel irony of unforgiveness is that it will not just wreck our relationship with the person we are bitter toward. It will infect and cripple "many," including those we care about the most.

That is why Dad wasn't able to love Mom like he wanted to during those early years of their marriage before I was born. She was his dream girl. But because he hadn't worked through and released his hurt and bitterness, there was a corrosive trickle down effect from his past that undermined his relationship with the person he loved the most.

Holding onto our wounds as a justification for refusing to forgive or reconcile with our dads not only keeps us limping through life, but we then begin to wound others. As the truism puts it well, hurt people hurt people. Without forgiveness, the worst elements of our personal histories will repeat themselves. The self-proclaimed victim in one generation becomes the villain of the next. Is it costly to request and grant forgiveness? Yes. But, failing to do so is infinitely more costly. Bitterness is nothing more than a shortcut to bondage. Forgiveness is the key to healing and release.

One of the verses that we sons sometimes aim at our fathers is Colossians 3:21, which says, "Fathers, do not embitter your children, or they will become discouraged." But notice what this verse has to say to us as sons. The Apostle Paul is warning us that bitterness toward our fathers will steal our courage.

For a young man, there are few possessions more vital and worth fighting for than the qualities of courage and strength of heart. To embrace bitterness against our fathers is to let some of our stores of courage and strength slip through our fingers.

When things are tough between our dads and us, we may tell ourselves that we don't need them in our lives anyway. But God designed our hearts to be in relationship with them. So if your dad is living, improving your relationship with him should be one of your highest priorities.

Dad Entered My World

I have loved building forts from the earliest days of my childhood—forts of all shapes and sizes. When I was six, my favorite fort was one I set up in the ruined foundation of the old brick carriage house behind our home in downtown Atlanta. I had picked up some of the bricks that slid into disordered piles on the ground and raised up the walls a layer or two to offer better protection against attacks from the local outlaws, otherwise known as my siblings.

When I was seven, we moved to Chattanooga, Tennessee, where my territory for boyhood battles and adventures dramatically expanded. We moved from the confines of a downtown neighborhood to an eight acre spread complete with meadows, woods, and creeks.

Convinced I had arrived in paradise, I threw myself into woodworking, carving, rock collecting, shooting at anything that moved with slingshots and bows and arrows, making wooden swords for dueling with my brothers, launching bikes off huge jumps when Mom was out running errands, playing little league baseball, wrestling, and of course, building forts.

Every new fort I built became more elaborate and involved, as did the name we gave the territory that surrounded it. I built a deep bunker fort beneath the Mushroom Tree, a stone-walled fort above the path by Tiger Paw Rock, a riverboat fort made of pallets in the creek bed near the Smoky Swamp, and a jungle fort in the middle of the thicket we called Indian Territory. All these culminated in my crowning achievement, a three-story treehouse made of oak and poplar trees I had cut down with Dad's axe, complete with water and electricity. Yeah, I was a pretty intense kid.

By the time I was twelve years old I had built twenty-two forts in all. This was my world. And except for my younger brothers, Matt and Josh, and my Golden Retriever, Prince Caspian the Great, it wasn't a world I readily shared with others. I was a loner and, as far as anyone could tell, I liked it that way.

Dad knew that if we were ever going to get past our conflicts, he couldn't just interact with me when he had to talk to me about my chores, grades, or temper. We had to strike up a friendship. To do that, he had to enter my world. So he began to help me with my projects and buy me lumber and tools.Best of all, he began to check out whatever latest fort I had just completed so he could rave about how cool it was. I ate it up! I loved giving tours and he loved seeing what I was up to.

He also started coming down to the wood shop we had set up in our garage to help me build birdhouses, sailboats, and swords—all the basic things that every boy needs in life. After putting in long hours in the office, working in clouds of dirt and sawdust with his allergies wasn't his favorite way to spend his Saturdays. But he knew that for me to get the message that he was interested in me and my life, he couldn't just express this to me in words. He had to show it to me by caring about what I cared about and doing with me the things I liked to do.

So for my five siblings and me, weekends became a time for projects and fun with Dad. We played baseball, went hiking, built fences for our dogs, turned spindles on the lathe for our front porch, went camping—whatever Dad could think of that we could do together.

Soon it began to sink in that, in addition to loving me, my dad liked me. For many kids, the phrase, "I love you" is just an empty statement you hear before you get disciplined or hear a lecture. But to know that your dad *likes* you is amazing. I received this message, not through the things he said to me, but because he showed me I was worth his time.

In Deuteronomy 6:5, we read this beautiful summary of what the core of relationship with God is all about: "Love the Lord your God with all your heart and with all your soul and with all your strength." Then the passage continues by addressing fathers, saying, "These commandments that I give you today are to be upon your hearts. Impress them on your children. Talk about them when you sit at home and when you walk along the road, when you lie down and when you get up."

My dad knew that to have a shot at having close relationships with us and passing on his passion for truly following Jesus in a culture like ours, he had to give us more than rules. Like this passage instructs, he had to blend his life with ours. He needed to give us his attention, to spend time with us, and to be fun and relaxed. He had to be the kind of guy we *wanted* to hang out with on the weekends. And he accomplished just that.

Dad Became My Biggest Fan

One day when I was twelve, I was pitching on the Signal Mountain All-Star Baseball Team, and we were playing our biggest rival, Lookout Mountain. That year I was throwing pretty fast for my age. So fast in fact, I accidentally stumbled upon something called a *curve ball*. When I would throw my fastball like I always had, it would go crazy places during the last ten feet before the plate. I realized I couldn't control it anymore, which really began to make me nervous.

My fastball had been my trademark, my specialty. Its speed and precision had made me an All-Star pitcher. But now something had changed. My greatest strength had become a wild card that I couldn't depend on. This happens to us as sons. Suddenly, something that has always worked for us and been under our control will no longer deliver, and everything we had built on that ability is shaken. We begin to wonder how much this loss of control is going to cost us.

With only a few innings left, being a one trick pony, I led off the inning with my fastball. Instead of zipping down the middle, though, it drilled the batter in the elbow, sending him off to first base crying. The second batter got up and halfway through the count I hit him in the helmet. I was red in the face, my pulse pounding, and my palms sweaty.

I avoided eye-contact with my coach as the third batter squared up at the plate. I stepped to the rubber, checked for the steal, and hurled the ball as straight down the middle as I knew how. The batter watched the ball as he took a huge swing, only to be struck by my pitch in the center of his chest! As the kid shuffled off to first, gasping for air, the umpire jumped up, threw off his mask and pointed straight at me yelling, *"You're outta here! Gimme another pitcher!!"* I walked off to center field, completely humiliated. Not only had I let down my team, but I'd also let down my pitching coach—Phil Downer.

After the game, I got into the car with my dad. I sat there in silence, tense as a steel trap, waiting to hear what he was going to say. But instead of hearing criticism, disappointment, or even a stream of advice on what I should have done, he said, "Son, did I ever tell you about the time I lost a case so big that the newspaper put my picture in the article instead of the guy's picture who won?"

"Seriously?" I said.

"Yep. I can't tell you how horrible I felt that day. I felt lower than turtle sweat!" he said with a laugh.

All the tension in the car was instantly gone. I knew without a doubt what my dad was saying. He was letting me know that even when I failed, I was good enough for him. I was OK. Even when I couldn't perform, achieve, or make him look good, he would be just as proud of me.

I can't tell you how many times I had seen my teammates' dads yell and scream at them from the bleachers until they dissolved into tears, their angry faces burning with shame. That day, in the midst of my failure, my dad communicated to me that he was on *my* team. I realized that I was unconditionally loved and absolutely accepted no matter what.

For many sons, this kind of knowledge is hard even to imagine. They can recite a whole list of the hoops they have to jump through to keep their dads happy. For them, being around their dads is about as much fun as going to the dentist, going to court, or being audited. Dad wanted this phase of our relationship to fade away. So he stopped being my critic and became my fan. My biggest fan.

Dad Invited My Honest Feedback

For centuries, historians have thought Napoleon Bonaparte died from stomach cancer or some other natural malady. But a few years ago, scientists decided to examine the chemical composition of a lock of his hair. After doing forensic testing, they discovered something surprising. His hair contained trace amounts of arsenic at levels that increased as it approached the scalp. At this point the arsenic was present in lethal levels. Contrary to popular belief, Napoleon hadn't died of natural causes. While on the island of St. Helena after his defeat at Waterloo, Napoleon had been poisoned!

Unbeknownst to him, something sinister had been put on his menu during the days and weeks before the French emperor's demise at the age of 52. Though it seemed harmless to him at the time, an element of his daily routine had become poisonous. The same thing can be true of us.

My dad knew that no matter how much progress we made in our relationship, there was a really good chance we would still rub each other the wrong way from time to time. He knew if I didn't feel free to be completely honest with him when our relationship began to fall into old patterns, our growing friendship would begin to wither without him even knowing it.

So he told me one day that, no matter how hard it might be, I needed to feel secure and welcome to share with him any constructive criticism I had about our relationship. This was risky for him because, like most people, he doesn't enjoy receiving criticism. But he knew that failing to open the lines of communication between us would only ensure that, if anything *was* poisoning our relationship, he would not find out about it until it was too late.

The day came in my early teens when my brother, Josh, and I took Dad up on his offer. In the abundance of our courage, we had Mom call him on his way home from work. She told him we needed to talk to him and that he had better be "prayed up," which was a family code meant that something tough was coming down the pike.

He got home and sat down at one end of the dining room table with Josh and me at the other. As we shared with him the ways we felt there was still pressure and tension in our relationships with him, he listened! I could tell it was hard for him to receive our comments. But he didn't defend himself or explain away our examples. He bit his tongue, wrote down what we had said, thanked us for our honesty, and said he would work on it. This was huge to us!

He could so easily have blown us out of the water with a counter attack, arguing that we had no idea how much he did for us or how good we had it in life. If he had done this and gone back on his word, our trust would have been broken. But because he received our constructive feedback, we knew we could depend on Dad to accept whatever hard things we needed to bring up and work through between us.

Dad Continued To Take His Hurts and Fears To God

From the earliest days of my childhood to the present time, my dad has been a faithful example to me of a man who consistently takes his burdens and struggles to God. The memories and experiences of a person's past do not always fade with time. As much as he wishes he could, my dad doesn't wake up in the morning to a clean slate. Often the first thoughts and emotions that wash over him are waves of pain, guilt, fear, and discouragement.

Dad has waged fierce battles with burdens and temptations I can hardly imagine, and he has broken through to a life of freedom and healing. But the secret to his great success has not been his military training or his willpower. His secret has been his unedited, deep, intimate relationship with Jesus Christ.

Morning after morning, throughout every year of my life, I have watched my dad take all the things that were swirling and throbbing inside him to the heart of God as it is revealed in His Word. Before Dad rushes into the rat race of his day, he unpacks the contents and pressures of his soul in the company of his Heavenly Father.

Rather than trying to take on home issues or his work load with an emotional cup already filled to the brim, he pours out his hurts and fears at the foot of the cross and replaces them with the most precious promises of God the Bible contains. Dad's devotional life has never been about impressing us or appeasing God. It has been a cherished time for him to enjoy being with the One who willingly took his place in death, the Friend who sticks closer than a brother.

Furthermore, my dad's life and my relationship with him have not been transformed merely because we worked so hard at it. Our efforts wouldn't have made a bit of difference if Dad hadn't brought his stresses, wounds and anxieties every morning to the only One capable of loving him perfectly. Then God worked in our lives to bring about reconciliation.

When I turned fourteen, I began to experience this kind of relationship with God for myself. I realized I had just been going through the motions in my faith and that it was time to make knowing and enjoying Jesus the central focus of my life. I began to follow Dad's example, spending regular time with God in His Word with the goal of walking more closely with Him.

Just like God was replacing Dad's hurt with security and sonship, so He also began to renovate and remake the shape of my life, both inside and out. I soon learned that because I was the unconditionally loved child of God, I didn't have to shoulder the burden of creating my own identity either as a maverick or a yes man. I could stop posing and pandering and just be myself.

By the end of high school, I noticed that my love for people was beginning to eclipse my love for projects. At the same time that my relationship with God began to grow, I discovered a passion for investing in and discipling other guys—the very same passion I had seen in my dad's life for so many years. I threw my life into new pursuits and began to notice that my struggles with anger and bitterness, against all odds, had virtually disappeared.

Dad Became My Life Coach

As my friendship with Dad grew, so did our conversations about life. When we would spend time together working around the house or going out for Mexican food, I discovered that my dad was a treasure trove of experiences, mistakes, lessons, and insights on just about every topic imaginable. I asked him about what it was like slugging it out in law practice as an up-and-coming attorney in Atlanta, what he learned leading men in combat, what things he wished he had done differently at my age, and what ideas and experiences he was most grateful had been a part of his life growing up.

I began to ask him for advice about dating, college, finances, career options, and people problems. We discussed contemporary issues of politics, economics, sports, and U.S. foreign policy. All the while Dad shared with me not only his view of the world, but also his view of me. He was living out Paul's comment to the Thessalonians, "We loved you so much that we were delighted to share with you not only the gospel of God but our lives as well, because you had become so dear to us" (1 Thess 2:8).

During our hang-out times together, our rambling conversations would often circle back to his sense of how God was shaping my heart, passions, gifts, and abilities, including what aspects of life and society I might be best suited. I could tell he wasn't just saying these things to push me to achieve or perform. His comments came out of the sincere respect that one man has toward another whom he accepts as his peer.

The honor of having my dad interact with me man-to-man was significant. It felt like receiving the final portion of a birthright. From then on, his advice and perspective on the subjects about which I was struggling and thinking about were a resource I sought out by reflex.

During my first two years at Bryan College, where I was studying Business Administration with plans to be a real estate developer, my friendship with Dad and his coaching role in my life were forged into a partnership as we began to share with others some of what God had taught us. Soon I began joining him at men's retreats and father-son events where we spoke together on the unlikely renovation God had brought about in the wreck of our relationship.

Halfway through college, I realized that though I wanted to be a developer, real estate no longer fascinated me. I wanted to be a part of God's constructive work in family relationships and in the lives of people. So I added a major in Bible and continued to invest in the lives of the guys around me on campus.

I began to take every opportunity I could to travel with Dad and learn more about how to encourage fathers and sons who were going through struggles that were similar to the ones we had experienced. When I graduated in 2005, I joined Dad in Discipleship Network of America full time where I am thrilled to say that God has already taken the passion He has given me for discipleship far beyond the horizons of what I had originally dreamed.

When I look back at where we have come from, the strong relationship that I have with my dad today seems like a miracle—and it is. When our relationship seemed like a lost cause, God accomplished what was humanly impossible.

Don't get me wrong, we still have to work at it. But the truth is, the only healthy relationships out there are the ones that are constantly being reviewed, reconciled, and worked on. Relational maintenance is a matter of survival. This world turns neglect into decay every time.

I once heard that the biological definition of death on a cellular level is when the body ceases to change. That makes a lot of sense to me. Change is a part of life, and it is part of vibrant relationships too. So now Dad and I change and grow and learn together. We hang out and talk and joke, asking the big questions of life, sharing thoughts with each other maybe others wouldn't understand.

Knowing my Dad is a lot of fun. Our friendship and partnership in the work we do together through DNA truly is a miracle. God has answered our prayers and done in us what we could never have done alone.

I am so grateful that He is still in the business of changing lives. Truly God "brings life to the dead and calls into being that which does not exist."

Questions For Reflection

1. What were some of the best and worst aspects of your childhood?

2. What was your relationship like with your dad?

3. During your childhood, would you say that you were more likely to be compliant or a non-conformist? In what ways?

4. When someone has wronged you, do you appreciate it when they are willing to admit it and make it right with you? What makes it hard for you to do this when you are the one in the wrong?

5. What is something you know you need to make right between you and your son or father?

6. What is one practical way you could "enter the world" of your son or father?

7. What is something in the life of your son or father which you could sincerely compliment or affirm?

8. Have you ever asked your son or father what you could work on to improve your relationship?

9. If you did, how do you think it would impact the level of trust and communication between you?

10. In what ways are you currently taking your hurts and fears to God? In what times or places do you feel the closest to God?

CHAPTER SEVEN

When Someone You Love is Wounded

by Susy Downer

Have you ever found yourself in a relationship with someone you cannot seem to understand, no matter how hard you try? Have you ever felt unable to anticipate and respond to the erratic attitudes, words, and actions of someone close to you? I have, and I know how exhausting and bewildering it can be.

You feel torn between a genuine love for the one hurting you and the fear that the hurt will only continue. You find yourself weighing in your mind the price of staying in the relationship against the cost of trying to leave it behind. But beyond these thoughts, two fundamental questions haunt you the most: Why is this person like this? Is it possible they could ever change?

Broken Dreams

Before Phil and I were married, we never argued—not even once. Everything seemed to be perfect. We loved spending time together on campus, going out for romantic dates, and talking about current events, politics, and the weighty issues of the world. He was funny and relaxed and loved me with all his heart. I had completely fallen in love with him as well.

After dating for a year and a half, I was confident that I knew him well. We seemed to have exactly the connection and spark I had always hoped for. The summer after our junior year of college, we were married. Suddenly, everything changed.

It was like some invisible switch had been thrown. On the second night of our honeymoon, seemingly out of nowhere, Phil's anger erupted like a volcano. It was the first time I had been yelled at in my entire life. The harder I tried to reason with him logically, the more angry he became. Finally, at a complete loss, I burst into tears. Seeing how hurt I was, Phil realized what he had done and began to calm down. As I cried myself to sleep that night, I asked myself in the darkness, *Who is this man I have married?*

As Phil has already shared, our marriage went steadily downhill from there. Without question, we had many good times. But they were not enough to take away the sting of the hard times in our relationship. As time passed, our conflicts and heated arguments continued with killing frequency. I, too, began to ask those two fundamental questions: *Why is Phil like this? Is it possible that he could ever change?*

After five years of struggling and coping, mostly on my own, I was at the end of my rope. For the first time in my life I was at a loss for what to do. I began to realize that the great sin in my life was not anger, but pride. From the time I was a little girl, I was always sure of what I wanted to do with my life. I believed that no one knew better than I did what choices I should make or who I should become. I was a planner, a doer, and an achiever—so I thought. But as I watched my ambitions and plans seemingly about to end in heartbreak only five years after my wedding day, I realized for the first time that my foundational sense of self-sufficiency was seriously flawed. Despite all my best efforts to solve the problems in my marriage, I was without answers and about to give up.

Then, just when I was on the brink of giving up and filing for divorce, something incredible happened: Phil and I discovered that it was possible for ordinary people like us to have a personal relationship with Jesus Christ. Having already realized that church alone and religious activities did not hold the answer, this was an unexpected development for us.

What shocked us the most was the practical difference that this new relationship with Christ began to make in our daily lives. It seemed like something or someone inside of us was bringing newness and wholeness into our lives where it had never been before. It turns out, that's exactly what was taking place. I now understood the genius in having Jesus Christ at the center of our marriage and making Him the one in control of my life. As my pride and independence began to give way over time to trust and obedience, I began to see that there could be no better plan for my life than the one God had for me.

Beginning Again

As Phil began to live as a follower of Christ, his life began to change right in front of me. When something would set off his temper, he would realize what he was doing, catch himself, and go into the other room to pray. To my grateful surprise, he would come back happy. Something miraculous was happening in his life!

With every passing day, Phil was becoming more and more the man with whom I thought I had fallen in love in the first place. As my love for him began to return and develop a depth I had never known before, I knew that something miraculous was at work in my life as well. I began to dare to hope that the answer to my second question was: *Yes, lasting change in my marriage was possible!*

Phil's growth toward self-control and an even temperament didn't happen overnight, however. It was a process that gradually unfolded. As I watched Phil work diligently to grow in self-control during this time, I began to realize how very little I actually understood the underlying causes of his tension, short fuse, and mood swings.

It occurred to me that if I were ever to move from loving him despite his challenges, to loving him in and through them, I probably needed to change some things in my life and attitude as well. So almost 35 years ago, I committed myself to looking for ways to grow in my role as Phil's wife, friend, and life partner.

When I think about how absolutely wonderful our marriage is now, and how beautiful the love is that we share, I shudder to think how close we came to throwing it all away. The road to healing for us has been a long one. But along the way, God has guided, sustained, and nurtured us at every turn. He has taught us how to understand and love each other all over again.

In reality, the love that He has built out of the ruins of our hurt and brokenness far surpasses the shallow, superficial love on which we based our decision to marry. When I look at the six wonderful children God gave us after He began restoring our marriage, I am overwhelmed with gratefulness to Him for what He has done, remembering Psalm 127:1, which says, "Unless the Lord builds the house, they labor in vain who build it."

Like I was, you may be in a marriage that is in turmoil. Or perhaps the troubled relationship in your life is with a child, a coworker, or a close friend. Whatever the case may be, I offer you my story. Though some of the details of your situation may differ from mine, I believe that the core dynamics of relational brokenness and healing remain constant.

As I share with you my mistakes along with the insights, lessons, and strategies I have come across during these years, my hope is that you will come away equipped, encouraged, and refreshed by the knowledge that there truly are answers to be found and reasons for hope.

Seeing What Lies Beneath

Far worse than a broken heart is a broken will. No matter how badly you have been treated, please do not buy the idea that it must all be your fault. When our arguments were at their worst, I used to wonder what was wrong with me. Yet, on the other hand, Phil's attacks seemed so illogical, I couldn't believe they were my fault. And, for the most part, anthey weren't. False guilt can steal your joy and your ability to see a situation clearly.

If there is someone in your life who has been through some kind of trauma that rears its ugly head in the form of controlling or abusive behavior, know that you are not the cause. You have inadvertently become the target of friendly fire. Whether your loved one has experienced battlefield combat or simply grew up in a home where the fighting never seemed to stop, you are experiencing the emotional fallout of those conflicts long ago.

When an earthquake strikes, the natural response of any person is to run for safety. But as terrifying as swaying buildings and roadways can be, we all nevertheless recognize that these are not the causes of what is going on. They are the symptoms. Beneath the upheaval and the churning terrain on the earth's surface, there are massive breaches in the earth's crust that we call fault lines.

Many years ago, before any of this was known, earthquakes no doubt seemed random and inexplicable, much like Phil's anger seemed to me early on. But eventually, the field of plate tectonics was born, bringing to us a fact of both scientific and relational significance: upheaval on the surface is almost always caused by brokenness underneath.

During Phil's childhood years and the months in the jungles of Viet Nam, Phil experienced a long list of horribly traumatic experiences. Despite the passing of time, the wounds these experiences left behind continued to impact him every day, even years later.

Because my childhood was virtually free of significant pain, I had little capacity for understanding how long old hurts can linger. Eventually, however, I began to see the connection between the visible tension and fears in Phil's life and the wounds from his past that lay beneath them. For me, this realization was crucial. It was the beginning of many lessons that would completely change my view of Phil and my role in our relationship.

Maybe like me, the turmoil between you and your loved one has made you react instinctively, pulling back from him or her out of self-protection. Perhaps your patience has run out, and you have begun to become entrenched in a growing sense of outrage at the way you are being treated. Believe me, I know what that pain and outrage feels like. Without question, there are some situations that simply should not be endured in passiveness or silence.

But let me encourage you that if the experiences you have undergone have caused you to disengage from your loved one, please, take a moment to reconsider your role in this relationship. I believe that for the vast majority of us in broken, painful relationships, God wants to use us as His agents of grace, love, and radical restoration in our loved one's life.

Much to my surprise, I have seen God work through me in Phil's life in powerful ways. Once I began to see that much of the hurt that Phil was causing me was due to the hurt he had undergone in his past, I began to see him through different eyes. I began to be more capable than ever of viewing him with the love and affection of Jesus. Despite the fact that it still took some time for us to work through our relationship problems, I began to reengage with Phil, and God began to rebuild our relationship and our love for each other in ways that brought back to life the fun in our friendship and the joy in our marriage.

Finding Support

In Romans 12:5, the Apostle Paul encourages us to depend on one another, knowing that "we, who are many, are one body in Christ, and individually members one of another." If there is someone close to you who is wounded, and especially if that person is in your immediate family, you need support. Period. Please do not try to live out your role in this relationship alone. Isolation is one of the most dangerous traps we can fall into.

This is especially true when trying to love someone through the after effects of what a broken, fallen world has done to them. If your trust has ever been violated or if you feel embarrassed by your situation, I understand it can be hard to open up to others. But I encourage you to find at least one person whom you can trust with what you are going through. During those early years, if I had not had the friendship, advice, and support of my first Christian friend and mentor, Liane Day, I don't think I would have made it.

Loving someone through the pain in their life can be a vulnerable, costly, and daunting task. But there is no more crucial or heroic thing you could do than to refuse to give up on them. Your loyalty in their lives will be the ultimate gift to them, ensuring that their worst fear – being left to wrestle with the bondage of their issues alone – will never come true.

Once I discovered the hope and strength that came from knowing Christ, this was the path I was committed to following, no matter the cost. Sometimes on a daily basis, I began to offer to God my hopes for healing in our lives and my fear that this healing might not take place. I prayed with Liane that God would continue to work in Phil's heart and bring a whole new spiritual quality of life and freedom to his actions, emotions, thoughts, and even to his memories.

During the time between when I began to pray and when I began to see Phil grow, I waited. I persevered. I was only able to do this because of the support I found in both my relationship with God and my friendship with Liane. If you find yourself hoping and struggling and waiting alone, please have the courage and vulnerability to find a friend or someone you look up to who can walk with you through this time in your life. Asking for help takes humility. But it is a noble humility, and nothing like the humiliation of ultimately facing loss and failure due to a refusal to ask for help.

While God is working in the life of the wounded ones close to us, let's not forget to allow Him to work in us as well. As God began a work of healing in Phil, He was also busy teaching dependence and trust to me. Now that He at last had the attention of both of us, the real change and growth could begin.

The Power of Forgiveness

Before I could be used as an agent of God's healing in Phil's life, I had to learn to live a life of uncompromising forgiveness. During my study of Scripture as a growing believer, I came across Colossians 3:13: "Bear with each other and forgive whatever grievances you may have against one another. Forgive as the Lord forgave you." This passage encouraged me in no uncertain terms to do the one thing I found most difficult to do: live in gracious and consistent forgiveness toward Phil.

After Phil and I would have an argument, my first instinct was not to extend words of grace and understanding. I felt compelled to explain, to defend, and to justify my words and actions. My desire to be understood was greater than my commitment to resolving our conflict. I just wanted him to acknowledge that his reaction was unjustified by what I had done or said.

After our conflicts, however, Phil usually wouldn't want to talk through or discuss our disagreement. He just wanted to move on. For this reason, at a very crucial juncture in our growing but still vulnerable marriage, I was faced with a decision that, at one time or another, we are all faced with: was I going to stand on what I thought were my "rights" or choose to forgive?

After experiencing over and over again the fact that defending myself only extended our conflicts, I finally began to submit my will to God and learn to forgive. Even when I haven't felt like it, I have tried to do my part in leading the way toward showing grace which invariably has melted Phil's heart as well.

Whenever I have found myself begrudging this simple act of grace in action, I try to remember the work of Jesus Christ for me on the cross. When all of us were deserving of punishment and death, Jesus demonstrated the gift of forgiveness and servanthood. He took upon Himself the full penalty of those who were still unrepentant, ungodly sinners, and enemies of God (Romans 5:6-10).

If you struggle with bitterness or resentment, or if you find it hard to forgive promptly when trying to resolve a relational conflict, remember that grace and forgiveness are what make relational restoration possible. Even Jesus did not attempt to reconcile us to Himself without it. How much more do we need to follow His example in the broken relationships in our lives.

Forgiveness is not easy, but it works. It is not common, but it produces an uncommon relational closeness and strength. If you are looking for something that will revive the relationships in your life beyond what you have dreamed, I can think of nothing greater than living a life of gracious forgiveness.

Moving Toward the Pain

Growing up, I rarely cried and rarely had anything to cry about. After meeting Phil, I found myself crying regularly. I had more grief from him in our first week of marriage than I'd ever had up to that point in my life. I'd never been yelled at before or been called names in anger. I had always been able to deal logically with my parents, knowing that they would listen to me and talk calmly through any disagreements we had until we came to a resolution.

Phil's reactions to certain things seemed anything but logical to me. When he would lose his temper and begin fuming over something I had done or said, I would be appalled. Then after fruitlessly trying to reason my way through Phil's emotions to what I thought was a rational view of things, I would give up and withdraw, often throwing myself back into my professional life with a new degree of underlying bewilderment and frustration that I kept buried inside. Phil was making less and less sense to me. I didn't know what it would take for me to begin to understand him.

In 1990, we met David and Teresa Ferguson of Intimate Life Ministries. We will never be able to calculate the profound benefit of the insightful and practical training we have received from these capable teachers and now dear friends. One of the biblical principles I learned from them revolutionized my view of emotion. It is found in Romans 12:15, which offers this simple piece of advice: "Weep with those who weep." There had been countless times since our marriage that I had found myself weeping about Phil, but not with him, and certainly not for him.

As I considered this passage, I eventually began to grasp the truth that the Apostle Paul is sharing here. He is encouraging us to comfort and share in the hurt of others by being willing to weep with them over the things that have brought them pain. The idea is that when one person enters into the fear, heaviness, or hardship of a loved one by sharing to some degree in those same emotions, they are able to receive a powerful kind of healing love through the companionship of one who is willing even to walk with them through the darkest things in their lives. Needless to say, this was a pretty radical concept for me.

I'm not someone who naturally has the strongest empathy reflex. As a matter of fact, in ninth grade I took a vocational test to see whether I should pursue my interest at the time of becoming a nurse. As it turned out, the only career choice the test said I was less cut out for than nursing was being a mortician! You are reading the words of someone who came into marriage with zero natural ability or inclination toward being a source of emotional comfort.

So it goes without saying that weeping with another person was not my typical mode of operation. I usually didn't even cry about my own problems; I just got busy working to fix or get past them. However, inexperienced as I was with taking on the role of a comforter, I was willing to learn.

I began to make it a point to ask Phil questions about the hardships of his childhood and serving in Viet Nam. As he shared the details of these experiences, I could see the hurt in his eyes. It took everything in me to avoid instinctively trying to correct or explain away his view of those experiences and the false guilt and anxiety they had produced in his life.

I bit my tongue and refrained from giving him advice, how-to's, or over-spiritualized platitudes. More than anything else, my goal was simply to sit with him, give him my full attention, and really, truly listen. Soon I began to see past the surface of his words to the images, experiences, sounds, and scenes he was describing. I began to be able to picture the scenes he so often relived in his head and actually feel the emotions from them that he was feeling.

As I allowed myself to enter into just a small part of the horrors he had experienced, tears started to come to my eyes. When he began to see how completely I was willing to join him in the loneliest, most wounded places in his soul, he began to cry as well. The space and safety for such times of honest self-disclosure are gifts that many hurting people are never given. It is so difficult to step out in servanthood and boldness to create such a place of safety.

This is not surprising, however. Often those who are in great pain express it in ways that hurt those who are closest to them, driving help away. That is how I reacted to Phil's wounds before I learned how to "weep with those who weep." I was pulling further away from him emotionally when I should have been moving closer to him.

When deep pain in a loved one's life shows itself on the surface by striking out in anger, manipulation, addiction, or depression, our tendency is to confront the symptom of the problem while overlooking the underlying cause. I cannot tell you how important it is for us to overcome this natural and detrimental response.

If we are ever going to be used by God to love and heal the hurting places in the lives of those around us who are wounded, it is imperative that we learn to move toward their pain during those times when we most feel like moving away. If we don't, we may spend the rest of our lives wrestling with, and running from, the turmoil on the surface rather than addressing the brokenness hidden beneath it.

To a hurting person, no explanation, how-to manual, or glib piece of advice can ever compare to your listening ears and flowing tears. They speak louder than words ever could that there is someone in their life who loves them enough to join them in those hidden places inside where they feel most injured and alone.

Showing Honor

In our culture, there isn't any glory in being deeply hurt. Dramatic stories can be interesting to people, but the pain that results from them rarely earns a person any special praise or status. Typically the opposite is true. Admitting the reality of how much a past experience still causes present heartache is something that many people find embarrassing. As people who have already suffered so much, it is a cruel irony that they so often feel pressured to bear in silence the continuing hurt they experience, adding the new ache of isolation and neglect to the old pain of past trauma.

In Romans 12:10, we are told to "Be devoted to one another in brotherly love; give preference to one another in honor." This passage encourages us not only to love each other, but to out-do one another in showing honor. If the loved one in your life has been through some kind of great tragedy, battle, or hardship, I encourage you to find any way you can to honor them.

I know it can be tempting to sit back and wait for them to begin showing you honor or respect first. But given what they have been through, they may need you to take the first step in this. No matter how small that step might be, it could jump-start you both into a new pattern of mutual honor and respect.

Even if the person close to you didn't play some particularly heroic or dramatic role in what they experienced, he or she will feel respected and cared for even by your choice to simply acknowledge how difficult their experiences must have been and how much you admire their efforts to deal with them since. Whether it was a war, a horrific car wreck, or a painful downsizing in their job, their past experiences have left behind pain that can leave a person feeling vulnerable, embarrassed, and perhaps even ashamed.

It can be difficult or seemingly impossible for them to communicate to you in a healthy way how great a need they have for your loving and respectful understanding in these painful places in their lives. That is why we have to be willing to see the signs of heartache that continue below the surface and take the initiative to minister to it on our own.

In addition to being willing to bring up and talk through the hardships they have undergone, I encourage you to look for a way to bring honor and credit to them, whether it's on Veteran's Day, Teacher Appreciation Day, Father's Day, or Mother's Day. Take time to write out words of encouragement and admiration, gratefully describing their most wonderful qualities and life accomplishments. As I have maintained this practice over the years, Phil has collected a personal treasury of notes, letters, voice mails, and gifts that remind him of how much love and honor I have for him. These gifts have meant the world to him.

Someone who has been deeply hurt may feel like a failure, useless, without value or purpose. The wounds they have experienced typically come along with destructive messages that assault their sense of identity and significance. Negative thoughts can be on a constant loop in their minds, such as, "I'm no good," "I'll never amount to something," or "Nobody would miss me if I were gone."

When you repeat words of honor and express your admiration and respect for your hurting loved one, you can be tremendously used by God to help restore proper thinking to their lives, replacing the lies that haunt them with the truth of who they are in your eyes and in God's.

Learning To Celebrate

We live in a time when the majority of us devote nearly every minute of our lives to activity and busyness of every imaginable kind. We do not weave time into our lives to take a break from the pace of modern life and "rejoice with one another" (Romans 12:15; 1 Corinthians 12:26).

As someone who feels very at home in the fast lane, working hard and staying busy, I'm always thinking about what needs to get done next, what I have forgotten, or what preparations I need to make for upcoming activities. Have you ever seen a bunch of beavers sitting proudly on a freshly built dam, throwing a party? I haven't. No matter how much they have already accomplished, they just move on to whatever project is next.

Many times, that's how I am and many years ago, that's how I was with almost no exception. I used to keep working on whatever was in front of me and, as soon as I finished, would move on to the next project or challenge. There is nothing wrong with having a bias toward activity, learning, work, and accomplishment. But if this tendency is not kept in check, it can cost us dearly.

When someone has been through a great deal of pain and has damaged emotions, taking time to enjoy, celebrate, and memorialize accomplishments and special events is like medicine to the soul. I began to learn to set aside evenings to spend with Phil for no other reason than to laugh and talk and enjoy a night out together.

When Phil was a young believer, he was discipled by a doctor named Jim Lyon who kept an appointment with him at a pancake restaurant every week. These times were not about criticizing Phil or reviewing a list of the things he needed to improve. They were about relationship. It was one time during the week when Phil had a person in his life who would express interest and care toward him without ulterior motives.

Phil always came away from those times of personal sharing and studying God's Word with a fresh sense of encouragement having experienced the camaraderie and care of a person who loved him enough to spend time with him without distractions or an agenda.

This is a practice that Phil subsequently carried over into our marriage. For many years now, our weekly date has been the most important event of our week. Soon Phil began spending weekly time one-on-one with each of our six children as well, despite the busy pace of our lives.

On our weekly date together, Phil and I find as many ways as we can to encourage each other, express gratefulness for the blessings in our lives and, in a word, celebrate. During these times I refrain from bringing up subjects related to our schedules, finances, projects around the house or other administrative-related issues. My goal is to multiply the joy in Phil's life by entering into it with him, describing to him all the things in our lives that I believe are going well, complimenting his strengths and accomplishments, and eagerly listening to him share with me the things he is especially enjoying or excited about.

The impact of these weekly times of fun and romance has been tremendous. As I take this time to devote my attention to celebrating him and the things in which he is finding joy that God has given us, I am helping to deepen and reinforce the happiness and sense of well-being in his life. We listen to each other, tell stories, update each other on the interesting things we have read or heard during the previous week, and generally just revel in the joy of each other's company.

These times of friendship, love, and celebration are healing for him. They push back the pain and darkness on the horizons of his life, illuminating his todays with a renewed awareness of how blessed we are, how proud of him I am, and how loved and worthy of honor and respect he is.

Dates are not just designed for Phil, though. They are tremendously important to me as well, and to my own sense of closeness with him. Ephesians 4:32 urges us to "Be kind to one another, tender-hearted. . . ." Phil takes this instruction seriously. He shares interesting things he has learned or done during the week that he knows I will enjoy hearing. In fact, over the last 35 years, he has made a practice of carrying a 3x5 card with him so that he can write down interesting things he has come across while on the road to share with me later on our dates. During his law firm days, he used to remind me that I am more important to him than his biggest client. He validated that statement by telling the receptionist that my calls were to be put through to him no matter who he was with or what he was doing. I still feel this sense of importance to him during our dates together.

Phil also makes sure that he takes a significant portion of our weekly time together to listen to me, to hear how I am doing and to ask how he can help. He will often ask me open-ended questions just to let me share my thoughts and express to him how I am doing, such as the following: What is hard in your life right now? How can I help? What is causing you stress? How can I encourage you?

When Phil asks me these questions, I know that he is inviting me to share with him whatever I am going through, struggling with, or thinking about. Our weekly dates have remained a treasured time for us of fun, celebration, and tender-hearted love.

A Lifestyle of Encouragement

1 Thessalonians 5:11 tells us to "Encourage one another and build each other up." This is clearly a call to action, not passiv-

ity. I've learned over the years that, as wonderful as Phil and my dates are, I need to notice and take advantage of the little opportunities to encourage Phil that come along throughout the week.

Especially for those of us whose loved ones have been deeply hurt, it is not going to be enough to "work this in" when we think of it or during a rough time. If we only encourage and verbally build up our loved ones when they are in crisis, we will only be helping them be "OK." However, if we proactively find frequent times to encourage them throughout a typical week, we can be a part of helping them gain brand new ground in their journey out of the darkness of their past.

Frankly, learning to practice this new skill was difficult for me. While Phil thrives on encouragement, I would much prefer a person's practical help as an expression of their care for me. It took me a long time to get to the place of consistently remembering how important encouragement is to Phil.

If your loved one is like Phil, I hope you will take from me the importance of being his or her cheerleader, faithfully noticing and commenting on the things in their lives that you admire or about which you are especially proud. If you think about it, you can probably come up with something positive or affirming to say to your loved one in almost any context.

If you have run out of meaningful and sincere things to say to your loved ones about who they are and how they are living their lives, you can always begin to share positive comments on what Phil calls "a global level." To Phil, it is very encouraging for me to share with him general comments about how well he is doing or how happy I am with the life that we share together.

If you find it hard to come up with enough specific ways to be encouraging, you might find that simply expressing a positive, grateful, and contented outlook on life will feel like a burst of sunlight on a cloudy day. In return, Phil has learned that I am greatly helped and encouraged when he is willing to take 20 minutes to help me around the house or to run an errand for me on the way to an appointment. In a world where stresses and conflicts constantly press in around us, living a lifestyle of mutual encouragement is one of the best ways to keep the joy in a relationship alive and strong.

Fighting Fair

Even though Phil and I have continued growing in our relationship and learning what it means to live more and more every day in harmony with each other, we still have our bad days. Both of us are very strong-willed people, and we have clashes of personality and preference to this day. Like every relationship this side of heaven, ours is a work in progress and consistently challenges us to rely on God for the strength and grace to love each other the way He loves us.

In light of this, we have realized that we are better off if we plan ahead of time how we are going to handle clashes when they arise. Romans 12:16 says, "Be of the same mind toward one another." We decided to apply this verse by creating a list of boundaries to help us protect and move toward unity even during those times when our unity is most threatened. We call them the Rules of Engagement. They are a collection of things that we believe husbands and wives should agree never to contemplate, bring up, threaten, or do. They are as follows:

1. Past sins or failures

2. Past marriages or relationships

3. Raising your voice to intimidate

4. Swearing

5. Using size to intimidate

6. Threatening physically, emotionally, or spiritually

7. Having an affair

8. Divorce

9. Murder

10. Suicide

11. Sarcasm

12. Belittling speech

13. Pouting

14. Stomping off

15. Slamming doors

16. Vengefulness

17. Withholding affection

18. Arguing or accusing in front of your children or other people

19. Dominating a discussion unfairly

20. Deviating in any other way from the fruit of the Spirit: love, joy, peace, patience, kindness, goodness, gentleness, faithfulness, and self-control

As you would expect, at times, in the heat of an argument, we have broken some of these rules, but they have still given us a basis for backing off from conduct that we know is wrong and which only escalates tension. Sometimes, remembering these rules, Phil will stop and say that no matter how I had irritated him, it certainly did not warrant the way he reacted. Other times I am the one to interrupt myself and admit that I have not been living out my commitment to be loving toward Phil in thought, word, and deed.

After admitting where we have crossed the line, we are better able to talk through whatever issues we need to resolve in order to move on. Romans 14:13 encourages us not to judge one another. The Rules of Engagement evaluate each other's conduct for us so we don't have to. They enable us to return to a mutually agreed upon point of reference for keeping even the most touchy situations from getting out of control and adding new hurts to old ones.

Understanding Each Other's Needs

One issue that has been consistently difficult for Phil and me is that we disagree on how to handle clutter. For instance, we have completely different views on how to complete a messy project in the house. My view is that it is a total waste of time for me to clear and reorganize my desk in the middle of a project, especially once I finally have everything where I can find it.

If I clear off my desk at the end of every day, I will waste countless hours in the process. Phil has graciously indulged my preference on this. But I've also realized that if he can walk through the main part of the house toward the front door and see that the counters are clean, there are no dishes in the sink, and there are no stacks of paper and projects lying around, it gives him energy and a great sense of order in our home.

People who have been through traumatic experiences often have a strong need for order in their lives. Order gives them a sense that everything is okay and not in chaos or disarray. One downside to the layout of our house is that Phil has to walk by my work area to get to the ice machine to refill his glass in the morning. Many times it has been challenging for him to make his way through the seeming disorder of my project area before he has even had a chance to start his day.

So for Christmas one year I bought him a little ice machine to put under his desk in his study. I know that might sound extreme to some of you, but often in life, the key to living together in love and deference is serving each other in the details. When we receive one another, along with each other's quirks and needs, we communicate unconditional acceptance toward each other, including those areas of need and preference to which we are not able to relate.

Another important need in Phil's life I have tried to honor is his appreciation for being on time. Phil loves to tell the story of how we first met. He shares that the day he first saw me in economics class, he arrived to class a little bit early, and I came in a little bit late. The last time he said that at a marriage conference, he added that this was a practice that we have continued for almost 40 years!

Of course, my view is that I wasn't late since there was still plenty of time before the professor actually started the lecture. Furthermore, the last seats to be filled are always the seats up front, which is where I prefer to sit anyway. So I was actually right on time! The truth is that we haven't, and probably never will, naturally agree on the best approach to handling our schedules.

We finally decided to flex to each other's preferences depending on the context. If something is really important to him, such as a board of directors meeting or an airplane trip, I honor his timeframe. But if we are going out for a date or headed off to do something fun together, he has committed not to stand at the door drumming his fingers on the counter while I finish a few things needed to make the trip as efficient and worthwhile as it can be.

In other words, we have learned that honoring each other's needs requires living lives of mutual compromise. While compromising on matters of conscience is never justifiable, compromising on matters of preference is absolutely essential. Amos 3:3 says, "How can two walk together unless they are agreed?" Compromising on the minor issues of life truly can do wonders for bringing agreement and unity into a relationship.

The Business Side of Harmony

Romans 15:14 tells us that we should be able and willing to "admonish one another." For many of us, this is a tough assignment to carry out well. For many of us, confrontation is either something we avoid at all costs or that we carry out in a way that is hurtful. It becomes even more complicated if the person being confronted has been wounded.

In my experience, admonishing Phil has been difficult to do in a loving way due to the fact that his past hurts can make my comments of constructive criticism feel more painful than I intend them to be. Someone with a background like Phil's has recordings of failure playing in his head and memories of rejection carved on his heart.

This means, if I am not careful, my words of correction or feedback can sound like just one more voice telling him that he's not good enough. Then what could have been a helpful discussion becomes an emotionally-charged collision. Over the years, through a great deal of trial and error, we have developed a system for discussing the hard things between us in a way that helps us avoid misunderstandings.

We have realized that because we will always have areas of our lives and in our relationship we need to improve, as well as minor differences and preferences between us that need to be negotiated, we might as well set up a time to discuss these issues on a regular basis. This is what we call a Business Meeting. It keeps us from ignoring the differences or irritants between us until the tension surrounding them becomes like a pressure cooker. It also keeps us from randomly blurting out our comments of correction or constructive feedback at times when they would be hard to receive.

A Business Meeting is a time when, once a week or so, we give each other the freedom to raise ideas, issues or problems related to our relationship, our family, our finances, our schedules, our travel plans, or any other topic, without the anxiety that it will be received poorly. This helps us keep our commitment to each other never to challenge, criticize, or confront each other in front of anyone else, whether inside or outside the family. Adding an audience to a difficult discussion only multiplies the chances of a small issue becoming a huge one. If a person has damaged emotions or struggles with anger, choosing to raise difficult subjects only in the privacy of a Business Meeting is absolutely essential.

What's In a Name?

Romans 16:16 encourages us to greet one another with a holy kiss. I think this is telling us we should greet each other with a warmth and affection that has the unique quality of those whose lives have been specially set aside by the life and love of Jesus Christ. If you're like me, you might be surprised at how powerful this principle is once you apply it.

For many years in our marriage, I didn't give much thought to how I greeted Phil or how I welcomed him home from the office or from a business trip. Then one day he began to express some preference to me about how he would like me to address him. I had gotten into the habit of referring to him by various pet names. In my mind, these were terms of endearment. To Phil, however, my calling him my buddy, sweetheart, honey, and darling just sounded folksy.

To make matters worse, I sometimes used these same terms when talking to our children, which didn't make them seem set apart for him at all. So one day he asked me to simply refer to him by his name, Phil. This seemed to come out of the blue. But out of deference for him, I said I would. Soon I had changed my habits and no longer referred to him in ways that he couldn't appreciate.

All this might sound like a minor issue to you, but the fact is, as human beings, we can't always choose the things that annoy or delight us. Often there are details in our lives and relationships which are a big deal to us no matter how minor they might seem to others. Without question, I have handled poorly many situations like this between Phil and myself. But in this case, by the grace of God, I decided that if changing the way I addressed my husband could in any way increase his daily awareness of how important and special he is to me, then I would be willing to do so.

Soon, I also learned to stop whatever I was doing when he arrived home to greet him at the door and make him really feel how happy I was to see him. Because I was willing to receive Phil's constructive input and suggestions into these practical areas of our relationship, a whole collection of irritating points of contact between us each week became moments of warmth, welcome, and intimate communication.

The lessons I learned working through these subjects in my relationship with Phil are not limited to the context of marriage. Expressing the life and love of Christ toward those around us will often require each one of us to make fundamental changes to the ways we are used to speaking and behaving. It is a challenging and complex thing to truly love someone well.

No matter how much we may have in common with someone, we are each nevertheless fundamentally different people with unique backgrounds, perspectives, and needs. If we want to learn how to love, welcome, and greet those close to us with the affection of Christ, we must be willing to serve them even in the small things. As you demonstrate love toward your friend or child or spouse by showing this kind of deference toward them, they will be impressed that you see them as being so worthy of honor.

Removing The Barbs

Because Phil was so touched by my willingness to change some of my habits to love him better, he has been encouraged to do the same toward me. One of my preferences he has chosen to honor is to remove sarcasm from the communication in our family. Sarcasm is humor at someone else's expense. In my experience, there is almost always a barb or a grain of cruel truth in a sarcastic statement.

Phil has a wonderful sense of humor and has the ability to light up a room with his laughter and jovial spirit. But there came a time when I told him that his periodic use of sarcasm could be hurtful to me, and I asked him if he would be willing to take it out of our communication altogether. Though this was not natural or easy for him, he agreed.

Before I knew it, his sarcasm disappeared. Just as I had been willing to protect and honor his sense of self by the way I referred to him, in the same way, he too had been willing to change one of his habits of communication to cherish me in a way that meant the most to me.

Unite And Conquer

In our culture, we live life on the run. We rarely slow down even for our own sakes, much less for the benefit of someone else. 1 Corinthians 11:33 challenges us with this countercultural instruction: "Wait for one another." We tend to be individualistic and competitive, pursuing efficiency over relationship. Many years ago, Phil and I decided that we wanted to resist the tendency in our lives to divide and conquer. We wanted to make daily, practical choices that would foster unity and closeness between us in a world that so often pulls people apart.

So when we go to the grocery store, we try to walk from aisle to aisle together rather than splitting up the list and meeting at the checkout. When we are planning out our fall or spring schedule, we adjust our travel schedules to include and protect ample time together to make sure our activities and commitments do not produce space or distance between us. In a culture where projects can so often come before people, we have decided to make each other a higher priority than our activities, errands, or obligations.

I have seen more marriages, friendships, and parent-child relationships starved and derailed by the breakneck speed of life than I care to recount. We live in a time when most of us feel almost controlled by the urgency of the next thing we have to get done! Phil and I have found that when we worship God rather than the goal of being completely on top of every last area of our lives, we have the time and attentiveness to live in such a way that we love people and use things rather than the other way around.

A Life of Hope

As Phil and I have worked over the years to be teachable and open to the training and counsel of wise mentors, the Word of God, and the conviction and guidance of God Himself, we have seen our relationship become all the things we had always hoped it could be. To be sure, we still have to work through the typical conflicts and differences of everyday life. But the healing and growth and training that God has brought into our marriage now enable us to work through these times in a way that is healthy and constructive.

If you are in a relationship that is still a source of pain, struggle, and discouragement for you, I beg you not to give up. You are not alone! God is even now waiting for you to ask Him to bring His life and healing into your heart and the heart of your loved one.

When things are hard and you wonder if you are going to be able to make it, remember that God does not expect you to find in yourself the answers and strength necessary to make it. Unlike some people you may have encountered in your life, your heavenly Father is eager to lift you up when you are discouraged. He is not bothered when you bring your burdens to Him. Rather, He is complimented that you would trust Him enough to ask Him for comfort, wisdom, and help. In our culture, we tend to measure success in terms of human autonomy. God measures our success based on our dependence on Him, His Word, and those around us.

This is what it means to live a life of hope. If the task of loving the wounded one in your life seems overwhelming to you, remember that this task is not just yours. It belongs to God and to the circle of those around you that He has placed in your life. We are not called to live lives of isolated endurance and obedience. We are called to live each day out of a hope in God. If God had not intervened, working miracles in our lives, I know Phil and I would not have made it.

I have shared much with you in these pages regarding the part that is ours to play in this kind of relationship. But never forget that we do not ultimately bear the responsibility of whether or not our actions are fruitful. Our role is to live with our loved one with as much wisdom and tenderness and servant-heartedness as we are able, by the strength of God.

God then invites us to slow down, rest, and wait expectantly for Him to act. He says to us, "Cease striving and know that I am God." (Psalm 46:10) He invites us to live lives not only of obedience and love, but also of hope, remembering that, in the end, only the Great Physician can truly bring the healing we need most of all. As the words of Scripture put it so well:

> May your unfailing love rest upon us, O Lord,
> even as we put our hope in You.
>
> ~Psalm 33:22

> God is our refuge and strength,
> An ever-present help in trouble.
> Therefore we will not fear,
> Though the earth give way
> And the mountains fall
> Into the heart of the sea.
>
> ~Psalm 46:1-2

> Peace I leave with you; My peace I give you.
> I do not give to you as the world gives.
> Do not let your hearts be troubled and do not be afraid.
>
> ~John 14:27

> Being confident of this, that He who began a good work in you
> will carry it on to completion until the day of Christ Jesus.
>
> ~Philippians 1:6

Questions For Reflection

1. What is the relationship like between you and the hurting person in your life?

2. What kinds of negative behaviors do they struggle with? (i.e., anger, rage, anxiety, discouragement, depression, control, compulsiveness, blame, manipulation)

3. What connection do you think there might be between their negative behaviors and the pain of their past experiences?

4. Do you have someone in your life who offers you support, comfort, and wise counsel?

5. Which of the following do you think your friend or loved one desires most: to be respected, understood, accepted, forgiven, comforted, listened to, encouraged, affirmed?

6. How do you think your loved one would most appreciate you expressing what you have indicated above? For instance, would they feel most encouraged by spoken words of praise, public recognition, an affirming letter, time spent together, help with a need, or doing a fun activity?

7. What are some ways you could bring a sense of celebration and increased joy into their life?

8. Are there any negative patterns of interaction that you have slipped into in this relationship? If so, what?

9. What unique needs have you observed in your loved one's life?

10. What annoyances or points of tension could you remove from your life to decrease the conflict between the two of you?

11. Despite the difficulties of loving someone who is wounded, how effective are you at finding strength and ultimate hope in the love and faithfulness of God?

12. What are some ways you could find fresh comfort and hope in God in the midst of this relationship?

CHAPTER EIGHT

Steps to Peace
A Practical Guide

We haven't shared the story of our family to pat ourselves on the back, but to assure you there is hope. If you are living a life that seems to be missing something you can't define, know that there is fulfillment to be found in life. But you can't find it on your own.

Even if you don't struggle with the kind of deep-seated anger and hurt that plagued me for years, many tensions exist in modern-day life for all of us. In a world that moves so fast and offers so many uncertainties, everyone is looking for a source of assurance, strength, and identity. But like I did, many of us look for it in the wrong places.

To some, it might sound too simple to say that hope for peace and a new life can come through a personal relationship with Jesus Christ. But that is the truth and it is what I have experienced. As He said about Himself, "I am the way and the truth and the life. No one comes to the Father except through Me" (John 14:6). He not only shows us the way to heaven, but also how to enjoy a life that is abundant now (John 10:10).

If you have not responded to Christ and accepted His free gift of salvation and eternal life, there is no better time to do so than right now. Here are some simple, straightforward guidelines for how this personal relationship can become a reality in your life. Please read through them carefully. At the end is a suggested prayer you can follow, or you can use your own words. The important thing is to acknowledge your need of Him and ask the Lord to take control of your life. This is the decision that transformed my life, and I wholeheartedly recommend it to you.

Step 1: God's Purpose—Peace and Life.

God loves you and wants you to experience peace and life that is abundant and eternal.

The Bible says:

"...We have peace with God through our Lord Jesus Christ" (Romans 5:1).

"For God so loved the world, that He gave His only begotten Son, that whoever believes in Him should not perish, but have eternal life" (John 3:16).

"The thief comes only to steal, and kill, and destroy; I came that they might have life, and might have it abundantly" (John 10:10).

Since God planned for us to have peace and abundant life right now, why are most people not having this experience?

Step 2: Our Problem—Separation.

God created us in HIS own image to have an abundant life. But we have chosen instead to live for ourselves. We have disobeyed God and gone our own willful way. We still make this choice today. This results in spiritual separation from God.

The Bible says:

"For all have sinned and fall short of the glory of God." (Romans 3:23).

"For the wages of sin is death [separation from God], but the free gift of God is eternal life in Christ Jesus our Lord" (Romans 6:23).

In other words, our rebellion results in separation from God.

Through the ages, individuals have tried in many ways to bridge this gap on their own, without success. Our attempts will never solve our own condition.

The Bible says:

"There is a way which seems right to a man, but its end is the way of death" (Proverbs 14:12).

"But your iniquities have separated you from your God; your sins have hidden His face from you, so that He will not hear" (Isaiah 59:2).

There is only one remedy for this problem of separation.

Step 3: God's Remedy—The Cross.

Jesus Christ is the only answer to this problem. He died on the cross and rose from the grave, paying the penalty for our sin and bridging the gap between us and God.

The Bible says:

"For there is one God, and one mediator also between God and men, the man Christ Jesus" (1 Timothy 2:5).

"But God demonstrates His own love toward us, in that while we were yet sinners, Christ died for us" (Romans 5:8).

"Jesus said to him, "I am the way and the truth and the life. No one comes to the Father except through Me" (John 14:6).

God has provided the only way. We must make the choice.

Step 4: Our Response—Receive Christ.

We must *trust* Jesus Christ and receive Him *personally*. He is so eager to begin a relationship with you!

The Bible says:

"But as many as received Him, to them He gave the right to become children of God, even to those who believe in His name" (John 1:12).

". . .If you confess with your mouth Jesus as Lord, and believe in your heart that God raised Him from the dead, you shall be saved; for with the heart man believes, resulting in righteousness, and with the mouth he confesses, resulting in salvation" (Romans 10:9-10).

The question is, are you going man's way, meaning you are trapped in sin, rebellion, separation from God, frustration, guilt, or lack of purpose? Or have you crossed the bridge with Christ, meaning that you know God and His peace, forgiveness, and abundant and eternal life?

Is there any reason why you cannot receive Jesus Christ right now? He loves you so much! Here are the steps:

1. *Admit* your need. (I am a sinner.)

2. *Turn* from your sin. (Repent.)

3. *Believe* that Jesus Christ died for you on the cross and rose from the grave.

4. Through prayer, *invite* Jesus Christ to come in and control your life through the Holy Spirit. (Receive Him as Lord and Savior.)

Prayer is about more than saying words. It is about the attitude of your heart. If you desire to receive Christ, pray a prayer like the one below or in your own words.

What To Pray

Dear Jesus, I know that I am a sinner and need Your forgiveness. I believe that You died for me and for all my sins. I want to turn from my sins. I now invite You to come into my heart and life. I trust You as my Lord and Savior.

If you prayed this prayer, then this is just the beginning of a wonderful new life in Christ! Here are things you can do that will help you grow in this new relationship with God:

Read your Bible every day to get to know Christ better.

Talk to God in prayer.

Seek fellowship with other Christians so you can grow in Christ together.

Tell others about your relationship with Christ.

Worship, fellowship, and serve with other Christians in a church where the Bible is preached and the love of God is genuinely lived out.

(Adapted from a booklet published by the Billy Graham Evangelistic Association. Reprinted with permission.)

Following Up

If you have just prayed the prayer above for the first time or renewed a commitment to God that you have made in the past, I hope you will take steps to grow in your relationship with Christ. The Discipleship Network of America offers a variety of resources that can help you get off to a strong start in your relationship with God. They are listed in the appendices.

A Spiritual Insurance Policy?

Some may think that salvation is some kind of spiritual insurance policy that keeps you out of the eternal fire of everlasting separation from God after you die. Given that someone else has paid the premiums, this would be quite a deal! While there is some truth to this idea, it does not tell the whole story. Salvation certainly does radically alter your eternal destination. A person who is saved has been given assurance of living life after death with God in heaven.

But if salvation only impacts one's eternal destination, then it really is just an insurance policy—a document in the file drawer of your life that has little practical relevance to how you live every day, sitting there until needed. Let's take a closer look at what salvation and having a personal relationship with God really means. Ignoring or misunderstanding something this huge would be a serious mistake.

There is no question that experiencing eternal salvation is a life-changing event. Receiving the good news that there is a solution for our guilt, shame, fear, and spiritual aloneness is huge news! It's more than a change of where we are going when we die. It's a dramatic change that takes place now on the inside of our lives and hearts. But what exactly has happened in my heart now that I'm saved? It's a good question.

Have you ever noticed that, even though we might disagree on how to define it, pretty much everyone has a sense of justice? All we have to do is think back to how we felt the last time we were wronged, and it's easy to remember the cry for justice that rose inside us.

On a personal level, I have always had some vague sense that, if there was a God, He should reward me sooner or later for the good things I have done. That was part of my idea of how justice and fairness should work. But it did not occur to me that it might work the other way, too. This was before I began a personal relationship with God. Soon, however, I bumped into the Ten Commandments.

As I began to truly understand them, I realized there was not one of them I had not broken, at least in my heart. This was very troubling. I began to wonder, "What if there really is a God, and what if this really is a summary of His Law? Am I accountable?

What if, when I die, I am brought into His court, and He knows even my secrets?" I shuddered. Crime has always been outrageous to me, and I have always thought there should be justice. But what about my crimes against my Creator?

Until this point, I had been living with a kind of uneasiness all of my life. Every one of us has an inborn moral compass called a conscience (Romans 2:14-16). We all have internal standards of right and wrong, and every one of us has violated those standards. That's why, when we take a good, hard look at ourselves, including our flaws and mistakes, we realize that on our own, we cannot hope to stand in innocence before a just and righteous God.

Your Life—The Movie

Imagine you are in a theatre jammed with people. As the lights grow dim, a major motion picture based on *your life* is about to begin. "All right!" you say. "My time in the spotlight has finally come. There should be some great stuff in this. . . ." You settle comfortably into your seat, but as the movie begins, you start to squirm. You discover there is a lot more here than you really wanted anyone to see.

It includes everything you've ever done, even when no one was looking and you thought you could get away with it. There is a soundtrack, too, that contains everything you've ever said, including your profanities, slander, gossip, road rage, angry outbursts at friends and family, secret thoughts, selfish motives, lust, vanity, and bitterness. Would you want to stay until the end of your movie and take a bow? I wouldn't.

But wait—there is good news! If you are saved, you have been *forgiven!* This means that the movie of your life has been completely edited by God. Because you have accepted what Christ did to remove all your sin, guilt, and shame at the cross, your heart and life before God are now perfectly clean. Everything about which you are rightfully ashamed has been entirely deleted from your life, permanently removed, thrown away. That's what it means to be justified. Consider how the following passages illuminate and expand on what it means to have experienced salvation.

"You were washed [the stain of sin cleansed away], you were sanctified [set apart from sin, and to God], you were justified [all charges against you were dismissed] in the name of the Lord Jesus Christ and by the Spirit of our God" (1 Corinthians 6:11).

"For all have sinned and fall short of the glory of God, and are justified freely by His grace [unearned favor] through the redemption that came by Christ Jesus. God presented Him as a sacrifice of atonement, through faith in His blood. He did this to demonstrate His justice, because in His forbearance He had left the sins committed beforehand unpunished—He did it to demonstrate His justice at the present time, so as to be just and the One who justifies those who have faith in Jesus" (Romans 3:23-26).

God cannot wink at sin. It is serious. It is in fact an act of ultimate treason against the One who created us and gave us every good thing in our lives. Because He is holy and righteous and just, He must deal honestly and thoroughly with sin. He cannot ignore it. However, because God is not only just and righteous, but also overflowing with kindness, grace, mercy, and love toward us, He paid the full penalty for our sin Himself in the person of His Son, Jesus, at the cross.

"But He was pierced for our transgressions, He was crushed for our iniquities; the punishment that brought us peace was upon Him, and by His wounds we are healed. We all, like sheep, have gone astray, each of us has turned to His own way; and the LORD has laid on Him the iniquity of us all" (Isaiah 53:5-6).

"God made Him who had no sin to be sin for us, so that in Him we might become the righteousness of God" (2 Corinthians 5:21).

Isn't that amazing?! What a shock it is that God would go to such extreme, costly, and painful lengths to bring us back into relationship with Him, despite all we have done to deserve His anger and all we have *not* done to earn His love. That's why salvation is described as a free gift. It is such an inexpressibly valuable gift and so undeserved, that anyone who receives it, and truly understands how precious it is, cannot help but live a life of gratefulness and love toward God because of His great love toward us. "He died for all, that those who live should no longer live for themselves but for Him who died for them and was raised again" (2 Corinthians 5:15).

Friend, let this sink in—if you have prayed a prayer to God for salvation, and you expressed it from your heart, then the charges against you have been dismissed! And it's not for lack of evidence. Your salvation and newfound harmony with God are not based on your goodness, but on the goodness and generosity of the One who stepped into your place. He paid the full penalty that justice had been demanding for you to pay, and He gave to you all the credit and benefits of His perfect record of goodness and right living. What a marvelous exchange!

So then, how should we respond to such a great rescue? Without a doubt, it is clear that we must not be content to grab it, file it away, and forget about it like an insurance policy. A person's salvation marks the beginning of a personal relationship with Christ. It is the beginning of a whole new life—life as it was always meant to be. It is a life that has become known as the life of a Christian.

What Does It Mean To Be a Christian?

The term "Christian" has come to have many different meanings over the centuries. Many of them are not accurate. In our country, often it is just another term for someone who does not identify themselves as belonging to a different religion. It is often used to describe someone who merely goes through the motions of going to church and acting religious.

But do you know where the word "Christian" originally came from and what it really means? Acts 11:26 tells us. It reads,

"The disciples were first called 'Christians' at Antioch." The term "Christian" here is another word for "disciple," a follower of Jesus. All "disciples" are "Christians," and all true "Christians" are "disciples."

What Does It Mean To Be A Disciple?

Being a disciple of Christ doesn't mean experiencing a burst of emotion, giving intellectual assent, or having a spiritual experience. It may include all of these, but it is much more. As one who has been saved, being a disciple of Christ means that a fundamental, life-changing decision for and commitment to Christ has been made. It means the Holy Spirit has come to dwell within a person to help change his or her desires, and to enable this new believer to have spiritual power to overcome temptation and sin.

A true, saving-faith decision to follow Christ as his disciple must not be based on emotions only (Matthew 13:20-21), or on intellect only (Matthew 13:22), but also upon a surrender of the will to the Lordship of Christ (Matthew 13:23, Galatians 2:20, Luke 9:23-25, Romans 6:2-8).

When Jesus called His disciples, we read that He chose them "that they might be with Him" (Mark 3:14). Salvation is not only about giving Jesus control of your life and obeying His teachings and will. It is not even just about coming to Jesus for forgiveness and new life. It is also about the beauty of deep companionship and friendship.

Look at how Jesus and His disciples interacted: they ate together, camped together, traveled together, went sailing together, and discussed ideas, issues, conflicts and life questions together. On top of this, Jesus taught them how to think about, and grapple with, the evil and hurt of this broken world. He taught them how to love others, how to stand up for the truth, and how to truly lead and serve and sacrifice.

Being Jesus' disciple means the same thing now that it did then. It requires a willingness to experience life with Him, to listen to His voice, to spend time with Him as you live your daily life, talking to Him honestly about what is on your mind and heart, and looking for His reply from the Bible and from His Spirit who now lives inside of you.

Being a disciple of Christ is holistic. It means a focus of life, a commitment of purpose, and a patterning of your life after the life of Jesus. It means you have embraced a teacher-student relationship that goes well beyond the confines of the classroom. It is about enjoying a relationship with Him and following His example and teachings as a matter of daily life.

A Disciple Will Obey Jesus' Word and Live In Freedom

Look up John 8:31-36 in your Bible. If you don't have one, either the NIV or NASB version of the Life Application Bible would be an excellent choice. Consider carefully what Jesus is teaching. Write out your thoughts below on what these phrases are intended to communicate. (I have used the NIV for these verses.)

- 8:31 "hold to": _____

- "teaching": _____

- "really [or, truly] my disciples": _____

- 8:32 "free" of what, or whom? (see verse 34)_____
  _____

Carefully read the following two passages and write down how they apply to you personally.

- Matthew 10:24-25: _____

- Luke 6:20 & 39-40: _____

- "We shall be like Him" (1 John 3:2) because we are "predestined to be conformed to the likeness of His Son" (Romans 8:29). That is our great comfort and hope!

Please look up the following passages and notice characteristics of being a disciple.

- Love for one another (John 13:33-35).

- A disciple's life is grounded in a deep, dependent connection to Christ (John 15:1-8).

Being A Disciple Does Not Mean We Never Fail Or Sin

Many people think they can earn salvation and must work to keep it by being perfect. This is not only false, it is impossible (Romans 3:20). We are saved by grace, and as believers, grace never ceases to be the anchor that grounds us in Christ. Out of this rootedness in the generous, gift-giving nature of God, a life of grateful obedience flows. Right actions do not earn or retain our salvation for us, but they do characterize the life of one who knows and walks with Christ. That is why it has been said that:

Faith alone saves, but faith is never alone (See Ephesians 2:8-10).

"Those who have the deepest appreciation of grace do not continue in sin. Moreover, fear produces the obedience of slaves: love engenders the obedience of sons." J.W. Sanderson Jr.

The Cost: Checking The Price Tags

Look up the following passages and jot down what you learn about singleness of purpose and wholeheartedness toward God.

- Luke 9:57-62: _____

_____

- Luke 14:25-35: _____

_____

- John 12:23-26: _____

_____

- Matthew 16:24-26: _____

_____

For further study, see also Galatians 2:20, 5:24-25, 6:14; Colossians 3:1-10; Romans 6:1-10; Philippians 1:21; and 2 Corinthians 5:17.

Why It Lasts Forever

A young bridegroom woke up one morning, and (unwisely!) said to his wife, "You know, Jen, it's funny. . . I really don't feel married."

"What's that supposed to mean?!" she replied, understandably miffed. "You are whether you feel like it or not!"

Thankfully, like marriage, the genuineness of our salvation is not based on how we feel on any given day. It is based on a binding commitment, just as marriage is. A promise is only as good as the person who has made it, of course. But in the case of our salvation, it is the God of the universe who makes the guarantee. Notice the work of God in salvation described in Romans 8:29-30. Can His work be undone?

Take a look at Romans 8:30-39. These verses explain that nothing in this life can separate us from God. Notice God's safeguards: "nor anything else in all creation," including the devil, ourselves, and even our own sins—past, present, and future. It's a good thing too, or else salvation wouldn't last for any of us!

As profoundly different as my life has been since I met Christ, I am far from perfect. Whenever I come to God asking for forgiveness, He is not angry or surprised. Psalm 103:14 says, "For He Himself knows our frame. . . ." He stands by the promise that He makes to all those who are His own: "I will never leave you or forsake you" (Deuteronomy 31:6) and "I am with you always, to the very end of the age" (Matthew 28:20).

Next, look at John 6:37-40. Here the Lord Jesus makes no requirement of those He is inviting to follow Him except that they "come to" Him. The phrase "will never drive away" is another conclusive statement! Never means never. "Eternal life" is not only an unimaginable quantity of life (a forever long time), it is an unimaginable quality of life—a kind of life that could only come from God.

The next passage to look at is John 10:27-29. Note that the command "follow me" refers to human perseverance (more on that later). In verse 28, "never perish" is a very strong statement in the original Greek language. It is a repeating negative and means this: "They shall not, in any way, perish; no, not for eternity." In verse 29, "no one" means not anyone (including yourself) or any being (including the devil).

Feel free to look up some of the following passages as well, and write phrases from the verses that belong in the two categories on the next page:

- Philippians 1:6, 2:12-13, 3:12-16

- 1 John 3:9

- Jude 21-24

- 2 Timothy 2:19

- Jude 1

- 1 Corinthians 1:8,9

- 1 Thessalonians 5:23-24

- Ephesians 1:13-14

- Romans 11:29

- 1 Corinthians 11:31-32

- James 5:19-20

God's Part: He Preserves Me	My Part: I Persevere In Following Him
_____	_____
_____	_____

A Matter of the Heart

Some people have said, "Now that I am saved, God will forgive me no matter what I do, so I can do anything I want." This kind of attitude shows something very wrong on a heart level. Christ came to "save His people from their sins," (Matthew 1:21), not for them. Why would a truly saved person make conscious decisions he or she knows will bring dishonor and sorrow to the very One who has given him or her every good thing in life, including a heart set free from guilt and made alive?

Scripture teaches us that to everyone who is truly saved and not just giving lip service, God gives "eternal life" (John 5:24) and it is an "eternal salvation" (Hebrews 5:9). If salvation could end, it couldn't be called "eternal." There are not two types of salvation, only one, and it is "eternal life."

Our salvation has been made possible through the unearned favor of God (Ephesians 2:8-9). With this renewal comes a new nature (1 John 3:9), and the Holy Spirit comes to permanently indwell the new child of God forever (John 14:16-17). No wonder people are changed and can truly be His disciples!

In this next section, I would like to lead you through a tour of some passages of Scripture that will help you gain a broader understanding of what it truly means to follow Jesus in a personal relationship with Him as His disciple.

The Importance of Good Spiritual Nutrition

No matter how independent we might think we are, taking in spiritual food is a matter of survival. Basic spiritual nutrition, which is easy to digest, is called the "pure milk of the Word" (1 Peter 2:2). As you continue to grow in this new life, you will be able to digest "solid food," the deeper truths of Scripture which are for the "mature" who are able to "distinguish good and evil" (Hebrews 5:11-13).

Don't settle for junk food—get the good stuff. It will be your "daily bread" (Matthew 6:11). Like food that sustains your body, this food will be life-giving to your soul (Isaiah 55:1-3). No matter how good the sermon is on Sunday morning, one meal a week is not enough.

Friend, please do not try to make this journey of faith alone. Is there a Christian person in your life that you respect? Can you summon the courage to ask this person to help you in your spiritual life? Take a moment to pray about it and see if the Lord brings someone to mind.

There are marvelous resources available to help you study God's Word, such as CBMC's "Operation Timothy," Walk Thru the Bible's "Daily Walk," and the Life Application Bible, mentioned earlier. You can learn more about these and other tools and resources in Appendices E and F. If you want to study a particular subject, ask your pastor or consult a Christian bookstore. If there is no one to help, begin reading the gospels, Matthew, Mark, Luke, and John. Then move on to the rest of the New Testament which will help you better understand the Old Testament later.

Also, never forget to ask God to continue to give you understanding. He does want you to understand! The Lord of the universe wants to talk to you. "Trust in the Lord and do good; Dwell in the land and cultivate faithfulness. Delight yourself in the Lord; and He will give you the desires of your heart. Commit your way to the Lord; Trust also in Him, and He will do it" (Psalm 37:3-5).

The foundation for right living is in the Book. It is the textbook of life, the "Manufacturer's Manual." In it, the Manufacturer gives instructions on how to assemble your life. When there are breakdowns, He will show you how to make the necessary repairs and adjustments. I believe the vast majority of God's will for your life can be found right in the Bible as the Holy Spirit illuminates it and shows you how to apply its truth in your specific circumstance.

So cry out to Him, "Show me your ways, O Lord, teach me your paths; guide me in your truth and teach me, for you are God my Savior, and my hope is in you all day long" (Psalm 25:4-5). Those "paths" mean that He will direct your life as you follow Him, one step at a time. "Teach me Your way, O Lord; lead me on a straight path" (Psalm 27:11).

Here is what the Bible says about itself in 2 Timothy 3:16: "All Scripture is God-breathed." This is the literal translation of this verse. You may ask, "But weren't there human authors?" Yes, and their unique personalities are apparent in their writings. Nevertheless, the Scriptures are the direct product of the creative breath of God and they say exactly what He had determined them to say from eternity. Thus, they are both fully human and fully divine, just like Jesus. Scripture is not a dusty relic from the past; it is a living book, and the Author Himself has promised to be present to help you understand what it means.

Therefore, as we read in Hebrews 4:12, it is no surprise that the Bible is "useful" for "teaching" (showing you the right path), "rebuking" (helping you realize when you've strayed off His path), for "correcting" (how to get back to the right path), and "training" (how to keep from aimlessly wandering off the path again) "in righteousness," because your Lord wants you to be "thoroughly equipped for every good work."

Jesus and the Bible

Anyone who calls him or herself a Christian (a follower of Christ) should also follow Him in His attitude toward Scripture. Jesus called it "the Word of God" (John 10:35). He affirmed that the writers were "speaking by the Holy Spirit" (Mark 12:36), who is God. He said that "the Scripture cannot be broken" (John 10:35), and He said that the Scriptures were so important that they would outlast the universe (Matthew 5:18-19, 24:35; Luke 16:16).

In fact, in the face of direct Satanic attack, Jesus relied on the Scriptures as His primary means of defense (Luke 4:1-13). He intended to set an example for us, because we too have this enemy!

Prayer: Talking To the God of the Universe

If you are like most of us, you would not be very comfortable walking up to a complete stranger on the street and trying to engage him in intimate conversation. Real communication takes place between people who have a relationship. Before we came to faith in Christ and began a personal relationship with Him, we were not on speaking terms with God. We were alienated, cut off by our own rebellion, independence, and sin.

Perhaps you know a lot about a famous person such as, for example, the President of the United States. You may even have read a book about him. But do you know him personally? Have you met him and spent some time in heart-to-heart conversation? Probably not. But that is exactly what the Creator of the universe desires with you—a close, personal relationship that begins now and lasts for eternity. He completely took on our human condition and fully identified with us. He says, "My sheep hear My voice, and I know them, and they follow Me" (John 10:27).

The Lord of the universe is not a thing, a force, or an it—He is a real person; an infinite, all-knowing, all-powerful, holy, and righteous person. He is so devoted to your well-being, He so deeply cares about what is best for you, that He gave His only Son so that a relationship with you could be possible. He already knows, and cares intimately, about every aspect of your life. You will be amazed at what He has said about that in Psalm 139! You have now entered into a personal relationship with Him and have been adopted into His family. That's right—you have become a member of His family! He wants us to begin to get to know Him like He knows us.

Prayer may seem awkward to you at first, just as it can be awkward talking to anyone else you have just met. But in any relationship, communication draws us closer. Talking, asking questions, listening for answers, expressing your thoughts, and sharing the deeper things that are really on your heart. . . that is what prayer is all about. It is not merely presenting your list of requests.

Without question, God answers prayer in incredibly power-ful ways! But prayer is also about what He does in you as you lead a life in conversation with the One who loves you most. Beyond the answers God will give you as you pray, the beauty of prayer is found in the ways it deepens your relationship with God over time.

Jesus Teaches His Disciples to Pray

Scripture has much to teach us about how to approach God in prayer. When the disciples asked Jesus to teach them to pray, He answered in this way:

> "This, then, is how you should pray: 'Our Father in heaven, hallowed be Your name, Your kingdom come, Your will be done on earth as it is in heaven. Give us today our daily bread. Forgive us our debts, as we also have forgiven our debtors. And lead us not into temp-tation, but deliver us from the evil one'" (Matthew 6:9-13).

Join me as we walk through this model prayer that Christ gave to us. My hope is that you will make these words your own and that you will learn to approach God intimately in prayer as this passage invites us to.

"Our Father"

This is a term of endearment, a word that means "my own dear father." Jesus is inviting His followers to address God with the same familiarity, security, and warmth that a child has toward a loving father.

"Hallowed"

This word means "made holy or reverenced." We are to ask God that His name, character, and nature, might always be set apart and special in our hearts and lives.

"Your kingdom come"

The idea here is that we are to live in such a way that we are used by God to extend His will and ways on this earth. We are to be those who build up, reconcile, comfort, protect, create, celebrate, encourage, discover, learn, shepherd, and beautify, all the good things which we find around ourselves that God has created.

"Give us our daily bread"

In the original Greek language, this phrase is in the present tense, meaning we should read it as saying, please "keep on giving" us what we really need. It is a prayer to God as our great Provider to continue to be the source of what we depend on in our lives.

"Forgive us our debts"

Here we are invited to request of God the gift of relational release from the guilt and burden of any of our sins. Even though we have ultimate and final forgiveness for all of our sins because of our acceptance of Christ's death on our behalf at the cross, we still have the ability to walk daily with Jesus or grieve Him. Though we will forever be free of any wrath due to our sins, we still must choose to turn from them when they creep into our lives, if we are to enjoy close fellowship with Christ.

"Lead us not into temptation"

This request humbly acknowledges that we are weak and prone to stray from the right path. Here we are to ask God to watch over us in a special way and guard us—body, mind, and soul—from the hollow allurements that only lead to the poisoning of our hearts and lives.

"Deliver us from the evil one"

With these final words, we are invited to ask for God's personal rescue in our lives from the schemes and destructive power of the enemy, Satan. Jesus has conquered sin and death and purchased us for Himself as His own precious possession. In a world that is under siege by the forces of evil, we are not left to slug it out alone. He eagerly waits for us to invite Him to be our source of protection, strength, and deliverance every day.

As a follower of Jesus, the life and adventure you have embarked upon is an epic one. It is filled with the greatest dangers and treasures imaginable. But if, instead of undertaking it alone, you rely on the provision of God, the wisdom of Scripture, the empowerment of the Holy Spirit, and the companionship of your new brothers and sisters in Christ, you will have every reason to be confident that the road you are walking will bring you safely home—home to a life, both now and forever, that is everything life was always meant to be.

Questions For Reflection

1. Where are you in your spiritual journey?

   - Would you say that you have begun a personal relationship with God?

- In Matthew 4:18-22, what does it mean to follow Jesus?

2. How does this apply to your life today?

3. As one who has chosen to believe in Christ and depend on His full payment on the cross for your guilt, what is wrong with living your life in order to earn your own salvation or be "good enough" to merit His love?

- If you had a gift that you were extremely excited about giving to someone, how would you take it if they responded by trying to pay you for it rather than gratefully receiving it?

4. Why do you think it is so natural and common for people to overlook God's free gift of salvation and new life in favor of trying to fix and improve their lives on their own?

- When and in what ways have you slipped into this way of thinking and behaving?

5. As the child of God, you are unconditionally accepted and loved by God—period! Your security in His love for you is unshakable. In light of this, which motivation for right living do you think is stronger and more lasting:

- Heartfelt gratefulness to Him for His goodness?

- A misplaced sense of guilt, obligation, and fear?

- Why?

6. In John 8:31, Jesus says "If you hold to my teaching, you are really my disciples" (NIV). "Abide in my Word, then you are truly disciples of mine" (NASB).

- Do you face any ideas, ways of thinking, or life patterns that compete with Jesus' teaching?

- If so, what?

- How do these affect you personally?

- Do they cause tension in your life and walk with Christ?

7. In John 8:32, Jesus talks about being "free."

- Does absolute freedom exist?

- Is this talking about being free to do whatever we want?

- What does Jesus mean by being "set free?"

- As one whom Christ has set free, what characteristics of being a disciple of Jesus are growing in your life?

- What are your areas of struggle and difficulty?

8. In John 13:34, Jesus says, "A new command I give you: love one another. As I have loved you, so you must love one another." How did Jesus love his disciples? Look for answers in these passages:

- 2 Corinthians 8:9: _____

  _____

- 1 Corinthians 13:4-8: _____

  _____

- John 15:12,13: _____

  _____

- Romans 5:8: _____

  _____

9. In Galatians 5:22-23, we read of the fruit that characterizes a life absorbed in dependence on the Holy Spirit.

- How have you sensed the quiet, still voice of God calling you to walk in tune with His Spirit?

- When have you recently recognized the nudge of the Spirit and followed His leading in a practical way?

- When have you resisted the voice and leading of God on a decision that seemed like it was no big deal?

10. In John 12:23-26, Jesus says, "The man who loves his life [cherishes it above all else] will lose it, and the man who hates his life [views it as being of lesser value in light of something else] in this world will keep it for eternal life." (See also Matt. 16:24-26.)

- In the end, does the person who embraces this truth and lives it out lose or gain lasting satisfaction?

- How does this apply to the decisions that you personally make in your professional life?

- In your social life?

- In your family life?

- In your leisure time?

DEDICATION

This book is dedicated to our ministry partners, Tom and Debby Coble, and to their family, whose passion is to live in such a way that others might come to experience the love, purpose, and lasting peace that come through knowing Jesus Christ. Their goal in supplying safety equipment through their business, Coble Trench Safety, is that "Everyone goes home every night," and their greatest desire in life is that everyone would experience a safe arrival to their eternal home through a personal faith in Christ.

The more I get to know Tom and his family, the more impressed I am with their commitment to using their energy, talents, and resources to serve and benefit people on a personal basis, through Coble Trench Safety, and far beyond. It is incredibly rare to see such a high standard of excellence, integrity, and servanthood lived out in such a life-encompassing, consistent way. We are so thankful for the friendship and partnership of Tom Coble and his family, and for their support of our mission to see people come to know Christ and live as His disciples.

Phil Downer

May 1, 2010

ACKNOWLEDGEMENTS

I want to express my great appreciation for two of my children who helped so intently and faithfully in making this book possible, Paul and Anna. Paul's writing, editing, and organizational ability have been absolutely crucial. I am so grateful for his willingness to take on this project, throwing his heart, life and experience into these pages. I also appreciate his willingness to transparently share his times of pain and victory as he has lived with someone who is a recovering sufferer of post-traumatic stress. Thank you, Paul, for the closeness we share and the wisdom you contribute to all we do.

Anna, in writing her chapter, has been so generous to share honestly her heart's struggle, walk with the Lord, and breakthrough to freedom and healing because of the Lord's touch on her life. What a joy it is to have a daughter with whom I have such a strong relationship and whose advice and wisdom I respect so much.

Paul and Anna, thank you so much for your love and friendship. I am so grateful for the joy it is for us to travel coast-to-coast, speaking and discipling together as a team.

I want to also thank my precious wife, Susy, for the willingness to forgive what others would have called unforgivable. She forgave, not because it felt good or because she wanted to, but because Jesus Christ called her to. Susy often mentions how incredibly glad she is that we "stuck with each other" when our life together was so difficult, broken, and painful. It has only been through the healing power and truth of our Lord Jesus Christ that our marriage has been so wonderfully revived and rebuilt over all these years.

The closeness we now share is almost incomprehensible as we look back on how we began. Thank you, Susy, for your undying faith in our Lord and love for me, for your constant servanthood and care for our family, and for your tireless commitment to the ministry God has given us, including the hundreds of hours you have spent on this book. Without you, in more ways than one, this book would never have been possible. You are my closest confidant and most precious partner in life. I love you more than words can say.

I also want to thank my dear friend, Doug Dickson, for his valuable contribution to Chapter 8. He first sent a draft of this chapter to me several years ago, which, along with the rest of this book, Paul has edited into this final form. Years ago, when Doug received Jesus Christ as Lord and Savior at thirty years of age, it became his consuming passion to know the Word of God and the God of the Word, and to share the Good News with others. Doug soon earned a reputation for spiritual maturity and professional excellence, earning a diploma from Grace Brethren Theological Practicum and serving twenty-two years in the business and professional world.

Doug then decided that his calling was to share the Good News with businessmen full-time. He is currently Metro Director in Columbus, Ohio for CBMC, a wonderfully effective outreach and discipleship ministry focused on business and professional men. Thank you, Doug, for your friendship and your contribution to this book.

We are grateful to our wonderful proof readers, Carol Arnold, Nancy Carlson, Jim Hand, Anne MacDonald, Don Mallas, Leinani Mikol, Marilyn Otto, Rob Otto, Larry Thompson, and

Mike Thornell, who were gracious enough to correct the final manuscript. Thank you, friends. You greatly improved the quality of this book and I am grateful.

Finally, I cannot overstate how transformed Susy's and my marriage has been due to the teaching, counsel, and friendship of David and Teresa Ferguson. Prominent and prolific authors, speakers, and counselors, David and Teresa first began to pour into our lives through their teachings twenty years ago. Since that time, we have had the privilege not only of working every day to apply the rich biblical principles they teach, but also to get to know them personally and co-write a book with them, *Unlimited Partnership: Building Intimacy and Teamwork Into Your Marriage.*

David and Teresa's life message of grounding each relationship in Great Commandment love has been the fundamental precursor to nearly every lesson we have learned about relationships, including those shared in this book. David and Teresa, along with your protégés, Bruce and Joyce Walker who have also ministered to us deeply, thank you for all that you have taught us, all that you have helped us through, and all the times of comfort, encouragement, and love you have shared with us over the years. You are truly choice couples and beloved teachers, modeling the way to lives of healthy relationships to countless people around the world.

Phil Downer

APPENDIX A

Note From The Authors

It is our privilege to serve you and the Lord in our common desire to be more Christ-like in marriage, family, church, work, and reaching others in a gentle and yet bold way with the love of Jesus Christ. God has called us to do this through Discipleship Network of America, a network of people committed to reaching and discipling others—serving pastors; all branches of the U. S. military, church, denominational and para-church leaders; men's ministries; the homeschool community; and individuals ministering in their homes and at work.

In all of our books, whether the focus is couples, men, family, or church, we address practical, everyday needs, challenges, questions, and hurts with biblical answers. Because we have experienced His ministry in our own lives, our family has not only been the crucible for life-change but also the medium through which we transparently share life's joys, tears, failures, blessings, and eternally significant relationships in a way that we trust will encourage, equip, and release you to be more completely one of His precious disciples.

We are available to share through live conferences, retreats, church services, military chapels, and seminars, in addition to speaking at outreach gatherings to those who do not yet have a personal relationship with Christ. We have captured much of this live material in various video and audio series presented either individually, as a couple, or with our children, who also share transparently the journey of our family.

Please consider us the friends next door or down the street who may be of some help or encouragement to you, your marriage, family, church, ministry or work as you answer God's call to see your life as a channel of His life-changing love and forgiveness as you build disciples.

Phil, Susy, Paul, and Anna Downer

APPENDIX B

About The Authors

Phil Downer serves as President of Discipleship Network of America (DNA). DNA is a nationwide network of people committed to following Christ's life of winning and discipling others to become disciple makers. The spiritual reproductive ministry of DNA flows out of the lives of people focused on Christ in their work, marriage, family, neighborhood, and church.

Phil is a popular national speaker at men's events such as Iron Sharpens Iron and Promise Keepers and speaks to all branches of the U. S. military at voluntary chapels on leadership, core values, and the truths he has learned that have transformed his life. Phil also speaks at couples events with his wife, Susy, and at family conferences with his six children. He has been featured twice on Focus On the Family and, along with Mike Wilkins, is the subject of Day of Discovery's 2010 documentary, "The War Within: Finding Hope For Post-Traumatic Stress. He is the author of *Eternal Impact: Investing in the Lives of Others, A Father's Reward – Raising Your Children to Walk in the Truth, Optimize Your Marriage, Just An Ordinary Man: Principles of Godly Leadership, Brave, Strong, and Tender,* and a coauthor of *From Hell To Eternity: Life After Trauma.* He and Susy are coauthors with David and Teresa Ferguson of *Unlimited Partnership: Building Intimacy & Teamwork Into Your Marriage.* Phil is also the editor and coauthor of *Effective Men's Ministry,* published by Zondervan.

A former machine gunner who served in Viet Nam with the United States Marine Corps in 1967 and 1968, Phil received a Bachelor of Business Administration from Southern Methodist University in 1972 and a Juris Doctor from Emory University School of Law in 1975. Phil was a successful lawyer before being led to Christ and discipled by fellow professionals. He left his position as senior partner of a 50-attorney law firm, with offices in Atlanta, Washington, Dallas, and San Diego, to serve as President of CBMC for a decade. Phil is on the Steering Committee of the National Coalition of Men's Ministries, a former elder of his church, and a member of CBMC. Phil can be reached at Phil@Downer.org.

Paul Downer serves as the Director of Operations for DNA Ministries and Managing Director of Eternal Impact Publishing. A coauthor of *From Hell To Eternity: Life After Trauma,* Paul travels the country with his father, Phil, and his sister, Anna, speaking at 2 to 3 conferences per month. He appears with Phil on their daily one-minute broadcast, *A Discipleship Moment,* which airs on over 550 stations in the United States and Canada.

Paul attended Bryan College as a Presidential Scholar where the faculty selected him from among his classmates three years in a row to receive the P.A. Boyd Award for Influence & Character.

After receiving academic awards from both Bible and Business departments, Paul graduated *magna cum laude* from Bryan College in 2005 with a B.A. in Bible and a B.S. in Business Administration. He is currently pursuing a Masters of Christian Studies degree from Regent College in Vancouver, British Columbia.

Paul has been a volunteer leader with Young Life for five years, mentoring high school students, speaking at their events, and meeting weekly with the guys he is discipling. He has been discipling young men one-on-one for 10 years and speaking with Phil for 12 years, including engagements in Peru and multiple events in Canada for Promise Keepers. Paul can be reached at Paul@Downer.org.

Anna Downer serves as the full time Field Staff Director of the DNA Young Women's Ministry with Discipleship Network of America and is a coauthor of *From Hell To Eternity: Life After Trauma.* A Presidential Scholar, Anna received the P. A. Boyd Award for Influence & Character and graduated *magna cum laude* from Bryan College in 2009 where she studied Spanish, Pre-Nursing and Bible. At Bryan College, Anna served as Vice President of her freshman class, a traveling presenter on the Worldview Team, and has been an adjunct speaker at conferences and conventions with Phil and Paul through DNA Ministries for eight years.

Susy Downer, a former attorney, served as legal counsel for Delta Air Lines for ten years, and was Assistant Corporate Secretary. She resigned her position with Delta in 1985, in order to devote herself full time to Phil and their children. Susy home-schooled their six children through high school. Three of them are now married. Abigail, 29, graduated from Covenant College and the University of Tennessee Law School. Paul, 27, graduated from Bryan College and is currently pursuing a Masters of Christian Studies from Regent College in Vancouver, BC. Matthew, 25, accepted a commission in the United States Marine Corps after graduating from Harvard College. Anna, 23, graduated from Bryan College. Joshua, 23, graduated from Harvard College, just completed his Masters from the London School of Economics and will attend law school in the fall. Susanna, 17, is finishing her junior year of home-schooling.

Susy is a coauthor of *Unlimited Partnership: Building Intimacy and Teamwork Into Your Marriage, Optimize Your Marriage: Making an Eternal Impact on Family and Friends*, and *From Hell To Eternity: Life After Trauma*. Susy speaks with Phil at marriage and family conferences and has appeared with Phil and various other family members on nationwide radio programs. Susy also appears in the 2010 Day of Discovery documentary, "The War Within: Finding Hope For Post-Traumatic Stress."

APPENDIX C

Conferences Offered by the Downers

Eternal Impact Conference

The Eternal Impact Weekend is a life-changing conference or retreat for men, couples, or families, which focuses on biblical principles of discipleship. Phil covers topics such as purity in marriage, healing brokenness, forgiving past offenses, seeing our marriages as our mission for intimacy and excellence, building deep relationships of influence and character, investing in our children, and overcoming stumbling blocks to discipling others inside and outside our families.

Session Titles:

1. Facing Your Chariots: From Brokenness to Healing

2. Oneness in Marriage Through Discipleship

3. Leaving a Godly Legacy—Discipling Your Children

4. Going Into The World and Making Disciples

Speaking References:

It is my privilege to provide the highest recommendation for the ministry of Phil Downer. Our church hosted a special men's event where Phil was our featured speaker. He also spoke during our multiple worship services on Sunday morning. I was deeply impressed with Phil's sensitivity to the needs of our local church and his willingness to provide Biblical insight into those issues. Phil demonstrates a genuine heart for God and people as he speaks. His practical insight into the issues of life resonates with his audience. You won't be disappointed.

~**Robert Fetterhoff**, Pastor, Grace Brethren Church, Wooster, OH

Phil Downer is a man of integrity and purity and has a unique message to men by the transparency of his own personal struggles. No speaker has ever been more candid and yet also helpful as Phil when it comes to sex. His testimony draws men to the power of Christ to change lives. He speaks about his happy marriage and gives very practical advice to husbands. I highly recommend him to your ministry.

~**Dr. Hayes Wicker**, Senior Pastor, First Baptist Church, Naples, FL

Phil's challenge to men to be disciple makers has greatly benefited my ministry.

~**Mike Winter,** CBMC Metro Director, Lansing, Michigan

[Phil's] true life stories integrated with rich Biblical truth help produce discipled men ... men of mature godly leadership.

~**Randy Weyeneth,** Major, USMC (Retired), The Navigators Military Ministry, Camp Pendleton, California

Phil Downer is a 'man's man.' He blends the rare combination of military toughness with genuine tenderness.

~**Dr. Bob Horner,** Senior Pastor, Peachtree Corners Baptist Church, Atlanta, Georgia

What a great experience! Phil's down-to-earth stories, personal vulnerability, biblical content and practical applications have touched us all!

~**Gene Getz,** Director, Center for Church Renewal, McKinney, Texas

Phil and Susy have been greatly used by God over the last twenty years.

~**Dr. Howard Hendricks,** Distinguished Professor, Chairman, Center for Christian Leadership, Dallas Theological Seminary, Dallas, Texas

Phil gave our men great encouragement and tools on how to spend time discipling their kids and other men.

~**Bruce Miller,** Senior Pastor, McKinney Fellowship Bible Church, McKinney, Texas

I have witnessed his brokenness and growth over the years.

~**Patrick Morley,** President, Man in the Mirror Ministries, Chairman of DNA Ministry Endorsement Committee, Orlando, Florida

Contact Information:

To view an immediate speaking sample, please take advantage of **our streaming video clips** which we have posted at the top right-hand corner of our website: www.Downer.org

For more information on having Phil and Paul speak at an Eternal Impact Conference in your town, church or discipleship group, please contact the DNA office at (423) 886-6362 or email Phil Downer at phil@dnaministries.org.

High School Leadership Conference

Paul and Anna are passionate about communicating to today's high school students the life-changing truths and strategies they have discovered over the years for how teenagers can live life to the fullest for Christ in our contemporary world. Drawing on a rich understanding of Scripture, pop culture, and the broken world of American teenagers, Paul and Anna speak with relevance and conviction to the greatest needs and most burning questions of high school students. Speaking at both Christian and public high schools, this dynamic speaking team is willing and eager to tailor their presentations to the audience in question. Below are some of the many presentations they offer.

Session Titles

By Paul:

1. Resolving Conflicts & Building Strong Parent-Teen Relationships

2. Escaping The Three Deadliest Traps Of Secular Culture

3. Top Challenges of a High School Graduate

4. Living Counter-Culturally in an Entertainment-Saturated Society

5. God's Radical Definition of Masculinity: Five Life-Changing Lessons from Jesus

By Anna:

1. What A Girl Needs to Know Most About Guys

2. What A Guy Needs to Know Most About Girls

3. God's Design & A Girl's Fractured Identity

4. The Truths, Secrets, and Choices that Make a Girl's Heart Come Alive!

5. Drawing Near to the Heart of God as A Teenager

Speaking References:

Paul was dynamic, engaged, and connected with the audience. He does a terrific job sharing godly principles with application to daily life in a way that is both clear and compelling. I highly recommend Paul Downer as a speaker at your conference.

~**Dick Honaker,** Trial Attorney

Paul and Anna gave us fresh inspiration that young people can lead godly lives in a perverse world. They set a phenomenal example that our students can follow. They love God wholeheartedly, speak with honesty, and are extremely effective at capturing and holding an audience's attention. Their handling of Scripture was extremely relevant and their personal illustrations helped the students relate and connect.

~**Vivian Welkner,** Dean of Women, Southside Christian School, Greenville, SC

Paul and Anna Downer are an extraordinary brother-sister team with an amazing story to tell. Their transparency in the telling, points us to a greater story, which ministers hope to all of us. The centrifugal force of life is spinning families apart; Paul and Anna describe the Biblical principles that kept their family together. They exemplify the old adage: God can take our mess and turn it into a message. I have caught a glimpse of Jesus through the window of their lives.

~**Renny Scott,** Headmaster, Christian Heritage School, Dalton, GA

Paul and Anna speak with clarity and a freshness of perspective that is memorable, integrating Scriptural principles with real-life situations. They did an excellent job! As speakers, these two are a refreshing change from the typical fare. Paul and Anna's teaching is rich with Scripture without being preachy. They are bluntly honest about their own struggles and share how our loving God can meet us wherever we are in life. They are a fantastic example of young Christians who have been through the struggles of the teenage years and come out on the other side with wisdom to share, tales to tell, regrets to use for examples and yet the joy of believers who are confident in the fact that God is in the proper place in their lives. Paul and Anna make sure to convey that God is in control, God loves us more that anyone, and we cannot replace our need for God with any other person, addiction, or relationship. We definitely want to have them back!

~**Kathi Millsaps**, Student Leadership Advisor, Crossroads Christian School, Birmingham, AL

Paul and Anna are honest and open – authentic! They were very credible with our teenagers.

~**Don Kauffman**, Principal, Southside Christian School, Greenville, SC

Paul and Anna are real, down to earth, and they connected with our students well. Their real-life illustrations and experiences grabbed our attention and made their presentations relevant. They related well to our audience because they both grew up in a Christian family that had to work through the same problems that we all face. They speak insightfully about how our culture's portrait of men and women is distorted from how they are presented in Scripture.

~**Robert Jones**, Upper School Assistant Principal, Southside Christian School, Greenville, SC

Anna and Paul really connected with us. They didn't just get up and lecture. They engaged us in discussion and helped us understand what we were hearing. They also spent time with us and talked with us one on one. I really felt that they were very real with a true heart for Christ. Listening to Paul and Anna talk was like listening to a friend share out of her life. They used Scripture in a way that was easy to understand and really made sense. They didn't sugar-coat things or talk down to us. Instead of saying "DO THIS," they said "Hey, here's how it is." And that was really cool. Paul and Anna gave us an awesome example of a Christian living in the real world dealing with for-real stuff. They were just plain groovy!

~**Miranda, Student**, Crossroads Christian School, Birmingham, AL

Contact Information:

For more information on having Paul and Anna speak at a high school, youth group, or parents group near you, please contact the DNA office at (423) 886-6362 or email Paul at paul@DNAministries.org or Anna at anna@DNAministries.org.

Brave, Strong & Tender Conference

This is a no-holds-barred seminar or retreat designed for men only or for fathers and sons. Drawing on the struggles of a difficult childhood, his combat experiences as a Marine machine gunner in Viet Nam, and the lessons he learned as he rose to become a managing partner of a 50 attorney law firm, Phil not only teaches but models God's ways of overcoming past struggles and becoming God's soldiers in the battle for our families, businesses, churches, and communities. This conference is strongly grounded in Scripture and deals with the challenging subjects of anger, lust, lack of vision, and growing in devotion to Christ. The men attending will be encouraged to follow our Lord and His Word in living out the victorious Christian life in their relationships at home, church and work.

Session Titles:

1. Gaining Victory over An Undisciplined Faith, Attitude, And Life

2. Developing The Disciplines To Be A One-Woman Man

3. Succeeding in Accountability in a David and Jonathan Relationship

4. Allowing God to Channel Himself Through Your Faith, Work, Church, and Life

5. A Call To Commitment: Changing the World One Person At a Time!

Speaking References:

Phil's life represents biblical principles put into action—what a remarkable testimony!

> ~**Don Mitchell**, Chairman of the Board, CBMC International, 2001-2005, Naples, Florida

Pastors should use Phil Downer for retreats, conferences and services.

~**Chuck Brewster,** Director of Honor Bound Men's Ministries, Assemblies of God, Springfield, Missouri

Personally I came away with the Lord giving me several reminders of how important my wife Kathy is to me.

~**Rob Harrell,** Senior Pastor, First Evangelical Free Church, Austin, Texas

Phil showed us how God connects generations of men who in turn have taken it to the next generations."

~**Dr. David Brown,** Minister of Discipleship, Ward Prebyterian Church, Northville, MI

I have had the opportunity of having Phil Downer speak to pastors and leaders. . . . He is one of the premier communicators in my experience in the men's movement.

~**Chris Van Brocklin,** Former National Director of Men's Ministry, Evangelical Free Church in America; Founder, Men With A Purpose

It is a joy to endorse them and their ministry.

~**Ron Blue,** President, Kingdom Advisors, Atlanta, Georgia

Contact Information:

To view an immediate speaking sample, please take advantage of <u>our streaming video clips</u> which we have posted at the top right-hand corner of our website: www.Downer.org

For more information on having Phil and Paul speak at a church or men's group near you, please contact the DNA office at (423) 886-6362 or email Phil at phil@dnaministries.org.

A Father's Reward
Parenting Conference

This is a conference specially tailored to address the most crucial issues facing the family today, packaged in a format that is vulnerable, practical, and easily transferable into your everyday life. Phil, Paul, and Anna (and others of the Downers as available) share from their real-life experiences the biblical lessons God has taught them in areas of character development, conflict resolution, building relationships, overcoming bad habits, dealing with bad attitudes, and gaining a vision to reach out to and impact those God has placed in your lives.

Session Titles:

1. Downer Family Testimonies - Finding Christ As a Family

2. Joyful & Fruitful Personal & Family Devotions

3. Father-Daughter Relationships - Foundations & Strategies

4. Anxiety, Discouragement, & Depression: Practical & Biblical Solutions

5. Insights on Dating Relationships, Singleness, & Counter-Cultural Identity

6. Hands Up: Surrendering Adult Children

7. Perfectionism, Grace & the Christian Family

8. Rediscovering the Life-Changing Person of Jesus

9. Solving Anger, Bitterness, the Sharp Tongue & Control

10. Rebuilding Relationships with Young & Adult Children

11. Discipling The Younger Generation: Strategies & Methods

12. A Call To Discipleship

Speaking References:

One of the best conferences I have ever hosted or attended was led by Phil and Paul Downer. We conducted a Family Life Conference which touched on the most important issues families face today. Phil and Paul were outstanding in the messages they shared and the manner in which they shared. They were very captivating and clear. Their messages were Bible based, compelling, and convicting. My staff and I whole-heartedly recommend DNA Ministries.

~Dr. Ron Dillon, Senior Pastor, First Baptist Church, Mt. Pleasant, NC

[Phil has a] practical insight into the issues of life. You won't be disappointed.

~Robert Fetterhoff, Pastor, Grace Brethren Church, Wooster, OH

Phil and Susy live ... with the humility and brokenness of people who have suffered with Christ and the joy and optimism of a couple who have experienced great growth and victory through their faith in our Lord.

~Bill and Ellen Armstrong, Former U.S. Senator, Businessman and Homemaker, Chairmen of the DNA Advisory Board, Denver, Colorado

Contact Information:

To view an immediate speaking sample, please take advantage of <u>our streaming video clips</u> which we have posted at the top right-hand corner of our website: www.Downer.org

For more information on having Phil, Paul and Anna speak at a church or conference near you, please contact the DNA office at (423) 886-6362 or email Phil at phil@dnaministries.org.

Unlimited Partnership Marriage Conference

This practical and powerful weekend conference shares how Phil's anger, selfishness, driven work style, and infidelity almost destroyed Phil and Susy's marriage—and how, against all odds, God restored it. Through insightful teaching from God's Word and vulnerable sharing from their personal lives, Phil and Susy communicate the keys to taking any marriage from merely surviving to thriving.

Session Titles:

1. Marriages Can Thrive, Not Just Survive

2. Intimacy and Communication In Marriage

3. Rebuilding Relationships, Healing Hurts

4. For Men Only: Practical and Biblical Steps to Living a Life of Purity

    For Married Women Only: A Wife's Role in Safeguarding Her Marriage

5. Establishing A Legacy For Generations

Speaking References:

The way he talked about his love for his wife and children brought tears to my eyes.

> ~**Don Collins**, Men's Ministry, Southview Baptist Church, Assignment Editor/Sports, USA TODAY, Reston, Virginia

[Phil] would enhance any ministry that would use his God-given talents of speaking.

> ~**David Townsend**, The Navigators Military Ministry, Camp Pendleton, California

Couples are still talking about the encouragement they received from our marriage weekend. It included the most practical instruction possible, because it came from transparent hearts of people who were willing to admit their mistakes ... publicly. Phil and Susy Downer's life message is that God can resurrect even the most hopeless marriage. They know first hand, because that's what He did with theirs.

> ~**Joe Tower**, Executive Director, Homeschool Building, Grand Rapids, MI

Contact Information:

To view an immediate speaking sample, please take advantage of **our streaming video clips** which we have posted at the top right-hand corner of our website: www.Downer.org

For more information on having Phil speak at a church or conference near you, please contact the DNA office at (423) 886-6362 or email Phil at phil@dnaministries.org.

State-Wide Education and Leadership Conference

Over the years, demand has only increased for Phil, Paul, and Anna Downer as speakers at state-wide education & leadership conferences such as those put on by FPEA (in Florida), NCHE (in North Carolina), CHEA (in California), CHAP (in Pennsylvania), APACHE (in Illinois), and many more. Their signature vulnerability, insight, humor, and Biblical grounding have enabled them to equip and encourage audiences across the country. As a multi-generational speaking team, the Downers are able to speak to the needs of the entire family from both the perspectives of parents and students. Below are listed just a few of the endorsements they have received from convention organizers over the past few years.

Speaking References:

Phil Downer's message for family discipleship is inspiring, essential, and enormously practical. I wish I had heard this message years ago. . . . I highly recommend Phil to you as a conference speaker.

> ~**Michael Farris**, Chairman of the Board & General Counsel, HSLDA

The Downers did an excellent job for our convention. They brought a powerful emphasis on parenting, which Phil also models practically through his family. We received very good responses from our attendees about their presentations, which were very supportive of the homeschool Mom and the homeschool movement. We would like to bring the Downers back in the future.

> -**Ernie Hodges**, President, North Carolinians for Home Education (NCHE)

I have personally seen how well the Downers relate to their audiences. . . . I am recommending that every father at our convention attend the Downers' sessions. I highly recommend the Downers as speakers to other homeschooling conferences.

~**Harry Beeson**, Board Member, California Home Education Association (CHEA)

Paul was dynamic, engaged, and connected with the audience. He does a terrific job sharing godly principles with application to daily life in a way that is both clear and compelling. I highly recommend Paul Downer as a speaker at your conference.

~**Dick Honaker**, trial attorney, homeschool dad, Board Member HSLDA

Discipleship begins at home and Phil and Susy have been faithful to God in raising their six children. They have also been faithful to share their experience with others, including their struggles, failures and hurts. Their practical insight in teaching and modeling spiritual truths to children has been a great encouragement to Anita and me, and to other members of our church's "Family Matters" class. We are thankful that through the ministry of DNA, others will be able to learn from Phil and Susy, as we have.

~**John Zeiser**, President and CEO, Southern Champion Tray Co., Signal Mountain, TN, DNA Advisory Board Member

Sessions By Phil:

1. Dad's Irreplaceable Role

2. Supporting and Encouraging the Homeschool Mom

3. Resolving Family Conflicts in Truth and Love

4. Developing a Plan for Sexual Purity in your Homeschool Family (For Moms and Dads and Young Men Age 13 and Up.)

5. Building Relationships with Peers and Parents

6. Giving Homeschool Teens a Vision to Change the World

7. Purity and Accountability for Fathers-Sons (The only workshop session that is NOT coed.)

8. Essential Elements of Building Teamwork and Vision

9. The Homeschool Marriage—From Surviving to Thriving!

10. Healing Wounds in a Family Between Generations

11. Leaving a Godly Legacy: Discipling Your Children

12. The Keys to Godly Discipline

13. Teaching Your Children How to Work with Godly Diligence

Sessions By Paul (Son, 27 yrs. old) or Phil and Paul (Father and Son)

1. Homeschooling the Strong-Willed Child – I Am One!

2. Resolving Conflicts & Building Strong Parent-Teen Relationships

3. Top Challenges of a Homeschool Graduate

4. What Is It Like To Be A Homeschool Student?

5. Media and Entertainment – Monitoring What Influences Your Family

6. Living Counter-Culturally in an Entertainment-Saturated Society (For Teen Conferences)

Sessions by Anna (Daughter, 23 yrs. old) or Phil and Anna (Father and Daughter)

1. What Your Daughter Wants & Needs From You Most of All (For parents)

2. Perfectionism & Grace in the Christian Family (For parents and teens, male & female)

3. What A Girl Needs to Know Most About Guys (For parents and teen girls)

4. What A Guy Needs to Know Most About Girls (For parents and teen guys)

5. God's Design & A Girl's Fractured Identity

6. The Truths, Secrets, and Choices that Make a Girl's Heart Come Alive!

7. How To Discover & Draw Near To the Heart of God As A Teenager

Leadership Sessions by Phil (For State and Local Homeschool Leaders)

1. Becoming A World-Changing Leader for Christ

2. Effective Leadership Teams in Homeschool Communities

Contact info:

To view an immediate speaking sample, please take advantage of **our streaming video clips** which we have posted at the top right-hand corner of our website: www.Downer.org

For more information on having Phil, Paul and Anna speak at a Leadership Training Conference in your town, church or discipleship group, please contact the DNA office at (423) 886-6362 or email Phil Downer at phil@dnaministries.org.

APPENDIX D

DNA
Military Ministry

Phil Downer is a combat veteran. He speaks nationally to all branches of the service on subjects of leadership, core values, and the importance of military training and service. He also shares his story at chapels, field chapels and voluntary military gatherings.

Speaking Recommendations

Investing in people is Phil Downer's passion. True life stories integrated with rich Biblical truth help produce discipled men and mature godly leadership. This is the need of the hour and what DNA is all about.

> ~**Randy Weyeneth,** Major, USMC (Retired), The Navigators Military Ministry, Camp Pendleton, California

I personally have the utmost regard for Phil Downer's presentation of discipleship and the Gospel. Phil spoke with competence on the subject and clearly communicated the gospel message with great illustrations bringing out the truths of the Scripture he shared. The audience hung on every word as he spoke. Phil's message to the students of the School of Infantry of the United States Marines was plainly understood. At the end of his message he gave an invitation to receive Christ and 17 Marines put their trust in Christ that evening.

Phil's speaking on discipleship at Camp Pendleton to the Navigator Military Ministry group encouraged the group to live for Christ and reach out to disciple others. The Marines loved what Phil shared and fully related to his life story. The Navigator Military Ministry group was deeply challenged in the area of discipleship.

With Phil's clear vision of the gospel and discipleship, he would enhance any ministry that would use his God given talents of speaking. Phil's use of his personal life and illustrations was key in communicating the gospel and discipleship.

> ~**David Townsend,** The Navigators Military Ministry, Camp Pendleton, California

I highly recommend Phil Downer to speak to military personnel. His message is compelling, biblical, and he relates well to the troops.

> ~**David Aspden,** Parris Island Gateway Director Military Ministry, Campus Crusade for Christ

Mr. Downer relates well to our Recruits and Marines. He encourages them in their training to stick with the difficult challenges they face. When speaking in a chapel setting, he describes how his faith has made a difference.

~Chaplain Steve Sexton, U.S. Marine Base Camp Pendleton

Military Biography of Speaker Phil Downer

Philip S. Downer

100 Downers Grove

Signal Mountain, TN 37377

President, Discipleship Network of America

Military Affiliation

- MCRD San Diego, Platoon 2214 – graduated October 1966
- Camp Pendleton School of Infantry – graduated November 1966

- Served with 2nd Battalion, 5th Marines, United States Marine Corps

- 1966-1968, machine gunner, Corporal

- 1967-1968, Republic of South Viet Nam, machine gunner with 2nd Battalion, 5th Marines

- Honorable discharge 1968

Family Military Background

- Son: 1st Lt Matthew Downer, commissioned November 30, 2007 - currently stationed at Camp Pendleton, California, 1st Recon Battalion.

- Father: LT JG United States Navy, served in World War II

- Grandfather: United States Army Air Corps, served in World War I, shot down in France.

Professional Background

- Southern Methodist University: graduated 1972 - BA in Business Administration

- Emory Law School: graduated 1975 – JD degree

- Hyatt & Rhoads Law firm: 1975-1990

- Christian Business Men's Committee: President 1991-2000

- Discipleship Network of America: Founder and President 2001 – current

- Ministry of the Year Award from National Coalition of Men's Ministries - 2007

- Core values and chapel speaker for Marines, Navy, Air Force, Army, and all denominations

- Recommendations from pastors and leaders from almost all denominations and church groups

Military Speaking

Since 2003, Phil Downer has spoken 123 times to over 40,000 members of the U.S. military. He presents motivational messages on the value of military service in building character, integrity, and teamwork in chapel settings. For voluntary formations, he shares the story of his Christian faith. He has spoken on Marine and Navy bases and to Cadets of the U.S. Military Academy at West Point.

Phil relates how the discipline he learned on the parade deck at MCRD San Diego saved his life when carrying out ambushes in Viet Nam, when he had to stay awake, be attentive, not move, and have the discipline to overcome the temptation to move, scratch, or wiggle that would have given away his position. He makes the statement that while he did not always understand all of the purposes his drill instructors were attempting to achieve at MCRD, he realized later that their training kept him alive in Viet Nam, and wished he could find those men and thank them for what they did in his life. He describes the value he received from the teamwork in the military, having been an unfaithful college "flunk-out" prior to joining. He encourages the Recruits to do their best, because their service will be respected in all fields of employment and future endeavors.

Letters of Recommendation

From Dudley C. Johnson, CMDR, CHC, USN (Ret.)

I give my highest recommendation to Phil Downer, who served as a machine gunner in the 2nd Battalion, 5th Marines, United States Marine Corps. Mr. Downer, who is now a lay minister and runs an organization called Discipleship Network of America, is an outstanding speaker. He spoke at the School Of Infantry when I was the Command Chaplain there, on character development and spiritual formation. I was in command there for three years – from 2001 to 2004 – and had him speak many times during that time to the Infantry Marines.

Also, he was the guest speaker at the 227th birthday celebration of the United States Navy Chaplain Corps for Southern California, for all area chaplains from all commands. Present in the audience were Maj. Gen. Bowden, Commanding General of Camp Pendleton, Col. Dennis Judge, Operations Officer for the 1st Marine Expeditionary Force. Col. John Terrell, Commanding Officer of the School Of Infantry, and many other senior officers and senior chaplains, both active and retired. One was Jack Peters, who served 43 years in the Navy and spoke of Mr. Downer's presentation in the highest regards. All of the officers, with no exception, said it was the most outstanding speech they had ever heard given at the Navy Chaplain Corps' birthday celebration. It was very inspirational and positive, relating biblical values to the Navy Corps and Marine standards of conduct.

I give Mr. Downer my heartiest recommendation to speak at MCRD, Camp Pendleton, or the Naval Station in San Diego – any Navy or Marine Corps Command either in the United States or abroad.

Dudley C. Johnson, CMDR, CHC,
USN (Ret.)

From Ryan Rupe, LT, CHC, USNR

March 29, 2005

School of Infantry (West)

Camp Pendleton, CA

Dear Sir:

Mr. Phil Downer of Discipleship Network of America has come to the School of Infantry three times in the last two years and has spoken to several thousand students and staff about spirituality, character, ethics and marriage. His experience as a Marine in Viet Nam, as a lawyer, father of six and head of Discipleship Network of America gives him a unique ability to impact the lives of many young Marines.

Mr. Downer is a man of deep Christian faith who is committed to educating and inspiring young people to reach new heights of personal and professional achievement. An impressive speaker, he instantly commands the attention of any group large or small. I have personally accompanied Mr. Downer in many chapels and field chapels and am always amazed at how quickly he can size up his audience and extemporize his message. He has an enthusiastic and humble spirit and is always willing to go to one more place no matter how late to talk to Marines.

We will be hosting Phil again this May and I hope that he will continue to come to SOI for many years. The students and staff of this place love him and always enjoy his visits.

When the young men of SOI are preparing for combat and are in the midst of so many pressures and life choices, Phil's words of character and encouragement are appropriate and uplifting. I'm glad to have Phil as a friend, mentor and fellow servant of our Lord.

Ryan Rupe, LT, CHC
USNR

From Brian Shearer, LT, CHC, USN

February 2009

U.S. Navy Training Center—Great Lakes

Dear Sir,

Mr. Phil Downer has spoken on two weekends to our Navy personnel and is the most effective Christian speaker to military personnel I have ever heard. I unequivocally give him my highest recommendation as a speaker.

Brian Shearer, LT, CHC
USN

Further references may be obtained from:

- Michael S. (Steve) Sexton, LCDR, CHC, USN, Chaplain
- Gregorio E. Huerta, LT, CHC, USN, Chaplain
- William G. Perdue, CAPT, CHC, USN, 1st MARDIV Chaplain
- Michael A Green, LCDR, CHC, USN, Chaplain
- Michael Jacobs, Navigators Military Ministry, 1ST SGT USMC, Retired

DNA Resources

Books by Phil Downer

Eternal Impact
Investing in the Lives of Others

Successful people reach their goals.
Significant people change their world.

Would you like to make a positive impact on the world that will endure for countless generations, and into eternity? That kind of impact is made through life-on-life discipleship the way Christ practiced it - changing people one life at a time. This insightful and gripping book will help you:

• Build a discipleship relationship with another person

• Overcome the barriers of discipleship

- Select someone to become your spiritual mentor

- Select someone to disciple

- Ask the right questions and pick the right setting

- Equip others to become change agents in the world around them

Hardback, 413 pages, discussion questions included

Praise for *Eternal Impact:*

I can think of few people who are as well qualified as Phil Downer to write a book on a vital topic such as discipleship. Phil has modeled being both a disciple and a discipler ever since the day he came to know Christ personally. This book will benefit the Kingdom, and I recommend it enthusiastically.

~**Ron Blue**, President, Kingdom Advisors, Atlanta, Georgia

The principles from Eternal Impact for discipling men come directly from the methods that the Lord Jesus used with His disciples. Phil is living proof that the Master's strategy is still working two thousand years later.

~**Steve Farrar**, Men's Leadership Ministries, Frisco, Texas

Brave, Strong and Tender
In Everyday Spiritual Battles

Like it or not, men today are at war – and the stakes are eternal. These are times that demand courage, strength, and tenderness. In this powerful volume, Phil Downer discusses how men can:

- Gain victory, God's way, over an undisciplined faith, fleshly attitudes, and the challenges of life

- Be a man of courage and a loving leader, husband, and father

- Develop an attitude of self-control and gentleness

- Establish accountability relationships

- Understand God's desire to work through his family, work, church, and life

- Cultivate a passion to leave a lasting legacy through discipling his children, grandchildren, friends, and neighbors

Hardback, 375 pages, discussion questions included

Praise for *Brave, Strong and Tender:*

This soldier's consuming passion is to walk with integrity before his Lord. He is a rock-solid, straight-shooting example we can follow. Brave, Strong and Tender is not just a book by Phil Downer - it IS Phil Downer. Grab hold of it and it will grab hold of you!

~**Pat Morley**, Founder and President, Man in the Mirror Ministries

Every man dreams of being brave in dangerous situations, strong in times of crisis, yet tender in his dealings with others. But for most of us, it remains just that - a dream. If you've been waiting for a resource that can help you take the next step toward maturity in Christ, Brave, Strong and Tender is the book you've been looking for.

~**Howard Hendricks**, Distinguished Professor, Dallas Theological Seminary

A Father's Reward

Raising Your Children To Walk In The Truth

As a father of six, Phil Downer knows and understands the challenge of raising godly children in an ungodly world. Phil and his wife, Susy, have poured real-life examples and rich biblical teaching into this dynamic book on transformational parenting. You'll learn how to:

- Build loving relationships with your sons and daughters

- Create family memories that promote closeness and trust

- Impact your children with fun and effective family devotions

- Meaningfully include your children in special projects and everyday events

- Help your kids find God's wisdom in ordinary situations

- Prepare your children to impact the world for Christ

Hardback, 366 pages, discussion questions included

Praise for *A Father's Reward*:

If you could spend an evening with Phil Downer and his family, play games with his children, dine with them in their home, or sit and talk with them in their rooms as I have, you would not only purchase A Father's Reward, you'd make it your mission to get it in the hands of every parent you know. I want every family in America - in the world - to read A Father's Reward. There is a way to turn our nation around, and it begins in the home. Not only will this book give you a vision, it will show you how that vision can become a reality.

~Kay Arthur, Executive Director, Precept Ministries

Just An Ordinary Man
The Principles of Godly Leadership

Do you ever feel common, inadequate, or unappreciated? At one time or another, we all do. But these are exactly the moments during which God wants to intervene and empower and equip us to become His representatives. From great struggles emerge great leaders.

This book will inspire you to become just such a leader. Its primary illustration comes from the life of a man who struggled with a difficult childhood, low self-esteem, and poor reading and writing skills. Yet, when surrendered to God, Gene Ast found the ingredients for greatness.

In the words of his wife, Earlene, he was "just an ordinary man." Yet God used him in an extraordinary way. Gene deeply touched everyone he knew while employing his business genius to mechanize a worldwide export industry. You will laugh, be encouraged, grow in vision, and be challenged to embrace a fresh approach to your life and sphere of influence as you walk through the remarkable life story of Gene Ast.

Paperback, 187 pages

Effective Men's Ministry

Developing and fine-tuning a thriving men's ministry takes perseverance, but it will pay huge dividends in the health of your church and its families. *Effective Men's Ministry* gives you the tools you need to start smart and stay strong.

Here is information you can really use—right away and for years to come. Created by the National Coalition of Men's Ministries, this comprehensive handbook takes you through the five stages of building a powerful, life-changing men's ministry in your church. Contributors include prominent pastors and men's leaders such as Pat Morley, Ed Cole, Haman Cross, Phil Downer, Steven Farrar, Jack Hayford, Dan Erickson, Steve Sonderman, Vince D'Acchioli, Chuck Stecker, and Willie Richardson. This volume is a rare and powerful collection of experience and insight on how you can bring the men of your church together in a bond of purpose, heart, and spirit. Includes worksheets, exercises, and sidebars.

Phil Downer, Editor
Paperback, 247 pages

Books by Phil & Susy Downer

Unlimited Partnership
Building Teamwork & Intimacy
Into Your Marriage

What is *the key to effective ministry?*

What is the key to maximizing the impact of your life?

What is the key to satisfaction, fulfillment, and joy?

*What is the key to experiencing the abundant life
Christ promised?*

Relationships. Not just shallow, patronizing relationships, but deep, intimate relationships with God and with others.

Discipleship Network of America and Intimate Life Ministries have teamed up to provide you with this invaluable resource for building close relationships, starting with the two most important: our relationships with God and with our spouse. Use this book for individual study, as a couple, or in a variety of group settings for men, women, and couples. It is practical, thought provoking, and challenging. It will transform your life and ministry!

By Phil and Susy Downer and David and Teresa Ferguson

Hardback, 248 pages

Praise for *Unlimited Partnership:*

Anything written by Phil Downer has to be valuable simply on the basis of this man's life and the example of his family. We have much to learn from this close friend whom Jack and I deeply admire as a man of God, husband and father.

~**Kay Arthur,** Executive Director, Precept Ministries

Optimize Your Marriage
Making an Eternal Impact on Family and Friends

Phil and Susy Downer share from their hearts and lives on creating a more joyful and intimate marriage and the lasting heritage of building Christ into your children. This book includes a first-hand account of how God helped them overcome the selfishness, anger, and poor communication that nearly drove them to divorce court. Delve into *Optimize Your Marriage* for help in rebuilding relationships, overcoming past pain, operating your home in a loving and strategic way, finding the cornerstones of effective communication, building a great family team, and effectively reaching others for Christ.

By Phil and Susy Downer

Paperback, 264 pages

Praise for *Optimize Your Marriage:*

Without equivocation, I endorse the Downers' ministry and commend this must-read book to all those who desire to be godly parents, passing on a godly legacy.

~**Howard Hendricks**, Distinguished Professor, Dallas Theological Seminary

Book by Phil, Susy, Paul, and Anna Downer

From Hell To Eternity
Life After Trauma

This is the gripping, personal story of one family's struggle with the inner wounds left behind by war, the anger and fear produced by these wounds, and the incredible healing that God brought to them as He rebuilt and restored their family.

Phil shares what it was like fighting for his life in the jungles of Viet Nam at nineteen years old, unable to keep his buddies alive. Susy describes her feeling of helplessness as she watched her dreams of a strong, loving marriage crumble to pieces as a young bride. Phil and Susy then share the solutions they found that brought their marriage back from the brink of divorce and restored it to health and vibrancy.

In the second portion of this family's story, two of Phil and Susy's children, Paul and Anna, offer their personal journey, along with time-tested insights on how to reach the heart of a child who has been wounded by anger, fear, or control.

This practical and hope-filled resource has been designed for anyone who has experienced pain in their life and wants to heal and rebuild the broken relationships it has caused.

By Phil, Susy, Paul, and Anna Downer

Hardback, 230 pages

Praise for *From Hell To Eternity:*

Reading your book was emotional, affirming, and filled with many quiet "wow" moments. I think it should be in every PX, on every chaplain's desk, required reading for every psychologist and taught in every military psychology course at the Academies and in troop training. This book is an answer to a much overlooked need and has tremendous relevance to families, both with and without military backgrounds.

~Wife of a combat veteran West Point graduate

Multi-Media Resources

The Day of Discovery documentary, "The War Within: Finding Hope For Post-Traumatic Stress," is a gripping and personal inside-look at the impact of life trauma and the solutions that can lead a person toward healing. Featuring the lives of Phil Downer and Mike Wilkins as they return to their battlefields in Viet Nam, this documentary portrays in detail the high cost paid by those who experience the horrors of war and how they can begin to move toward recovery. Comprised of personal interviews and actual combat footage, "The War Within" will help anyone seeking real-life answers for the fallout from traumatic experiences either in their own life or in the life of someone close to them.

This DVD or any of the many other audio, video, or print resources offered by DNA can be ordered at www.DNAministries.org

APPENDIX F

Other Helpful Resources

America Family Online: www.afo.net, 850.362.6180. Improves Internet safety and accountability.

CBMC (Christian Business Men's Connection): www.CBMC. com, 800.566.2262. Committed to winning and discipling business and professional men; publishes both Operation Timothy discipleship material and the Living Proof DVD series, Lifestyle Evangelism and Lifestyle Discipleship.

Center for Relational Care: www.relationalcare.org, 877.567.5656. Helps couples, families, and single adults experience more meaningful relationships with God and one another through conferences, small group relational intensives, counseling, and training. Incredibly impacting for those in crisis or for those who desire to go deeper in their relationships.

Child Evangelism Fellowship (CEF): www.cefonline.com. 800.300.4033. Provides excellent training materials for evangelizing and discipling children, or setting up a Good News Club in your home.

Covenant Eyes: www.covenanteyes.com. 877.479.1119. Stores and sends all the websites that are visited from your computer to an accountability partner of your choice.

Crown Financial Ministries: www.Crown.org, 800.722.1976. Teaches God's people financial principles; Has effective resources for adults and children.

Day of Discovery: www.dod.org, 616.942.6770. Uses television to bring the hope and truth of God's Word into people's lives in a meaningful and relevant way.

Discipleship Network of America: www.DNAministries.org, 423.886.6362. DNA's vision is to win and disciple people to become disciple makers through marriage and family conferences, men's retreats, homeschool and church events, books, and DVDs.

ESword: www.esword.com. Free Bible software downloads.

Family Life: www.FamilyLife.com, 800.358.6329. Has a goal of saving marriages and families and provides excellent resources to support its vision.

Family Talk with Dr. James Dobson: www.MyFamilyTalk.com, 877.732.6825. A new radio ministry hosted by Dr. James Dobson and his son, Ryan. Current and previous broadcasts can also be heard online at www.oneplace.com/ministries/family-talk/listen

Focus on the Family: www.Family.org, 800.232.6459. Has an outstanding breadth of resources to assist in every kind of family issue.

God's World News: www.gwnews.com, 800.951.5437. Weekly newspapers for children, middle school, and adults assist in the development of a biblical world view for all aspects of life.

Help For My Life: www.HelpForMyLife.org. Honest and thought-provoking conversations on a variety of topics with a pastor, a counselor, and a friend.

IBLP: www.iblp.org, 630.323.9800. Dedicated to strengthening families.

Intimate Life Ministries: www. GreatCommandment.net, 800.881. 8008 Helps build relational ministry one marriage and family at a time with outstanding conferences and tools that equip people with skills to communicate and love God and each other.

iQuestions: www.iQuestions.com. Deals with topics ranging from marriage and parenting to money and career.

Iron Sharpens Iron: www.IronSharpensIron.net, 800.451.9239. Mobilizes regional ministries to resource local churches with first-class one-day equipping conferences for men.

Man in the Mirror: www.ManInTheMirror.org, 800.929.2536. Committed to engaging every man in America with a credible offer of Christ and with resources to grow.

Military Ministry: www.MilitaryMinistry.org, 800.444.6006. Equips churches for ministry to returning warriors, veterans, and their families.

Military Missions Network: www.MilitaryMissionsNetwork. com, A network of evangelical churches, chaplains, and parachurch ministries reaching, equipping and ministering to military members and families worldwide.

Moody Audio: www.moodyaudio.com, 800.626.1224. Provides resources for spiritual encouragement, growth and outreach. *Stories of Great Christians, Ranger Bill, Nature Corner, Sailor Sam,* and *Sugar Creek Gang,* available on MP3, are foundational and transforming for children.

National Coalition of Men's Ministries: www.NCMM.org, Committed to putting a discipling men's ministry in every willing church.

Officers' Christian Fellowship: www.ocfusa.org, Unites Christian officers for biblical fellowship and outreach, equipping and encouraging them to minister effectively in the military society.

Precept Ministries International: www.Precept.org, 800.763.8280. Dedicated to teaching people to study God's Word for themselves.

Revive Our Hearts: www.reviveourhearts.com, 800.569.5959. The teaching ministry of Nancy Leigh DeMoss, who has a deep burden for genuine revival among women.

RBC Ministries: www.rbc.org. Committed to teaching the Word of God so as to lead people of all nations to personal faith and maturity in Christ.

ScreenIt: www.screenit.com. Exhaustive review site for previewing the appropriateness of a movie's content. (Warning: reviews are very detailed, including those covering films with extreme content. Discretion is advised.)

Steve Farrar: Men's Leadership Ministries: www.SteveFarrar. com, 800-636-5323. The author of many books and a conference speaker, Steve's focus is equipping men for spiritual leadership.

Summit Ministries: www.summit.org, 866.786.6483. Provides summer camps for 16 – 21 year-olds to train servant leaders in worldview analysis, equipping them to champion the Christian faith, and inspiring them to love God with their hearts and minds.

TeenPact: www.teenpact.com, 888.343.1776. Trains young people to be leaders who will impact the nation and the world through a State Capitol Four-Day Class and other seminars and conferences.

The Navigators Military Ministry: www.MilNavs.com. Shepherds military men and women throughout a lifetime of deployments, relocations, and career changes with seamless connection both within and beyond the military.

Young Life: www.YoungLife.org, 877.438.9572. Reaches middle school, high school, and college students in friendship and hope with the message of Jesus Christ.

Your Story Hour: www.yourstoryhour.org, 800.987.7879. More than 500 stories available from Scripture, literature, history, and everyday life, teach character qualities while they entertain and inspire. Broadcast weekly online, by radio, and also available on CD.

Youth With A Mission (YWAM): www.ywam.org. 719.380.0505. A powerful youth training and mission organization equipping and sending out young people to spread the gospel around the world. Offers an excellent Personal Prayer Diary Daily Planner.

Discipleship Network of America
Field Staff Directors

Roy Abbott, Field Staff Director—Northern Illinois and Iowa
Office # (815) 589-3413
www.focalpointministries.net

Brian Ascherin, Field Staff Director—South Arizona
brianascherin@msn.com

Mike Behar, Field Staff Director—Central Florida
Office # (352) 307-1207
www.udministries.org

Ben Blackiston, Field Staff Director—Western Michigan
bblackiston@berriencenterbiblechurch.org

Dave Brown, Field Staff Director—Washington, DC Area
wacmm@comcast.net

Tom Cheshire, Field Staff Director—Southern Illinois
Office # (217) 566-3780 (home)
rpmfm.org

Mike Dobbins, Field Staff Director—San Diego, CA
mgdobbins@sbcglobal.net

Anna Downer, Field Staff Director—Young Women's Ministry
Office # (423) 886-6362
www.dnaministries.org

Paul Downer, Field Staff Director—Operations
Office # (423) 886-6362
www.dnaministries.org

Brian Doyle, Field Staff Director—New England
Office #(860) 233-8136
brian.doyle@ironsharpensiron.net

David Dusek, Field Staff Director—Southern Florida
DavidDusek@floridamenofintegrity.org

Dan Erickson, Field Staff Director—Kansas City, MO
www.peoplematterministries.com

Will Fox, Field Staff Director—New York
willfoxjr@rochester.rr.com

Jim Guth, Field Staff Director—Northern Florida
Office # (352) 371-6682
www.floridamenofintegrity.org

Alex Kettles, Field Staff Director—DNA Oregon
alexskettles@gmail.com

Jim Morud, Field Staff Director—DNA Northwest
Office # (503) 397-2688
www.dnanorthwest.org

Joe Nordstrom, Field Staff Director—DNA Midwest
Office # (952) 454-0210
joenordstrom@gmail.com

Steve Ollanketo, Field Staff Director—DNA North Central
steve.ollanketo@yahoo.com

David Parsons, Field Staff Director—Winston-Salem, NC
Office # (336) 793-0687
www.davidparsons.org

Andy Read, Field Staff Director—Fund Development
Office # (940) 759-5088
www.edmi.org

Bernie Ritterbush, Field Staff Director—Chattanooga, TN
Office # (423) 893-8885
www.mensministry.org

Darryl Sheggrud, Field Staff Director—Indiana
Office # (260) 459-7710
www.mensministrynetworkfw.com

Jeremy Sperring, Field Staff Director—Accounting
Office # 404-253-7518

Chris Van Brocklin, Field Staff Director
Men With a Purpose
Office # (410) 750-2888
www.menwithapurpose.org

Eddie Watkins, Field Staff Director—Raleigh, NC
Office # (919) 851-3117